KNIT TOGETHER

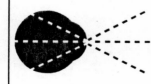

This Large Print Book carries the
Seal of Approval of N.A.V.H.

KNIT TOGETHER

DISCOVER GOD'S PATTERN FOR YOUR LIFE

DEBBIE MACOMBER

THORNDIKE PRESS

A part of Gale, Cengage Learning

GALE
CENGAGE Learning

Detroit • New York • San Francisco • New Haven, Conn • Waterville, Maine • London

Copyright © 2007 by Debbie Macomber.
The Acknowledgments on pages 383–384 constitute an extension of the coypright page.
Thorndike Press, a part of Gale, Cengage Learning.

Thorndike Press® Large Print Inspirational.
The text of this Large Print edition is unabridged.
Other aspects of the book may vary from the original edition.
Set in 16 pt. Plantin.
Printed on permanent paper.

LIBRARY OF CONGRESS CATALOGING-IN-PUBLICATION DATA

Macomber, Debbie.
    Knit together : discover God's pattern for your life / by
Debbie Macomber. — Large print ed.
        p. cm. — (Thorndike Press large print inspirational)
    Includes bibliographical references.
    ISBN-13: 978-1-4104-0798-6 (hardcover : alk. paper)
    ISBN-10: 1-4104-0798-5 (hardcover : alk. paper)
    ISBN-13: 978-1-59415-260-3 (softcover : alk. paper)
    ISBN-10: 1-59415-260-8 (softcover : alk. paper)
    1. Christian women—Religious life. 2. Large type books. I.
Title.
BV4527.M23 2008
248.8'43—dc22   2008023977

Published in 2008 by arrangement with FaithWords Hachette Book Group USA, Inc.

Printed in the United States of America
1 2 3 4 5 6 7 12 11 10 09 08

To Wendy Lawton
For seeing the vision long before I did

O LORD, you have searched me and you know me.
You know when I sit and when I rise;
you perceive my thoughts from afar.
You discern my going out and my lying down;
you are familiar with all my ways.
                    PSALM 139:1–3 NIV

CONTENTS

FOREWORD

BY LIZ CURTIS HIGGS

You are going to love Debbie Macomber.

She's the bubbly friend you've always hoped to meet and the savvy mentor you've longed to know. Though she calls herself "average in the most average of ways," you'll soon see how far *above* average Debbie truly is. A role model, a cheerleader, and a wise sister in Christ, she puts her heart on the page, revealing her numerous challenges and setbacks, as well as her many joys and triumphs. Her goal is to help *you* set goals; her dream is for *your* dreams to come true. In Debbie's vocabulary, *success* is another word for *blessing,* bestowed by a loving God who has called and equipped His followers to do great things.

A dozen years ago, when the Lord was nudging me toward writing fiction, one name was whispered up and down the halls of every writers conference I attended: Debbie Macomber. She was not only a hugely successful novelist, with sixty million (!) books in print, but she was also known for her strong faith in Christ. *That's* what really got my attention.

I finally worked up the nerve to introduce myself at a writers gathering and found a very approachable, unpretentious woman whose faith was genuine and whose enthusiasm was contagious. "So you're going to write historical fiction?" Debbie asked, without a hint of sarcasm. The sparkle in her eyes and warmth in her voice communicated not only, "I believe you," but even more so, "I believe *in* you" — a vital distinction.

Our conversation that morning blew me away. Most successful people enjoy touting their own accomplishments; Debbie wanted to know what *I* had in the works. Rather than looking over her shoulder for someone important to talk to, she fixed her gaze on me, nodding and listening as I poured out my dreams. Instead of treating me like a wannabe, she saw me as a gonnabe. Talk about a confidence booster!

Watching her in action over the years, I've discovered Debbie's secret: she greets everyone who crosses her path with the same affirming, upbeat approach. Encouraging others comes as naturally to her as breathing. Or storytelling. Or knitting.

You'll find that same joyful attitude in each chapter of *Knit Together,* her first nonfiction book. Searching for your God-given purpose in life? Debbie will point the way. Hoping to meet the real woman behind so many best-selling novels? You've come to the right place. Needing a positive word in a negative world? That's her specialty. Longing to see your own words in print? Debbie offers her secrets to writing and publishing success (*patience* tops the list!). Wondering if God can use you, whatever your talents might be? The answer (*yes!*) and all the necessary how-tos are waiting for you here.

You won't just meet Debbie the business-woman; you'll also meet her husband, Wayne, and the children and grandchildren she loves. You'll hear about friends from church and motivators from around the globe, stirring memories in your own heart of people, both unknown and well known, who've shaped your life.

Each real-life story Debbie shares is designed to turn your secret dreams into spoken dreams and your spoken dreams into reality. Along the way, she exposes the lies we often tell ourselves to avoid moving forward — "It's who you know" and "I'm too old" and "It's too hard" — then reminds

13

us that, if we know God, we're never too old, and nothing is too difficult for Him (Jeremiah 32:27; Luke 1:37). Such good news!

You'll note verses of Scripture woven throughout *Knit Together,* especially as the book draws to a close and focuses on our being "Created for Blessing" and "Created for Worship," my two favorite chapters. Her respect for the Bible is clear: "We were created to soak in it, inhale it, live it, *be* it."

Debbie's mission statement is captured in God's words addressed to Abraham: "you will be a blessing" (Genesis 12:2 NIV). I'm here to tell you, girlfriend — she's taken that promise and run with it! Blessing her loved ones. Blessing her neighbors. Blessing strangers in need. And in turn, blessing her readers. Oh, and did I mention she's just plain *fun* to be around? A whole chapter on the benefits of laughter says it all.

If you fear that pursuing your dreams might come at your family's expense, Debbie offers comforting examples to put your mind at ease. If you worry that success isn't pleasing to the Lord, Debbie gently dispels that notion with solid guidance from God's Word. If you can't imagine adding one more thing to your busy life, Debbie provides timesaving tips and practical tools for tak-

14

ing charge of your calendar.

Knit Together is a joy-filled reminder that we were created according to God's design and for His distinct pleasure. May your journey with Debbie Macomber open your eyes, open your heart, and open the door to a whole new way of loving God and serving others!

Celebrating two decades of professional speaking, Liz Curtis Higgs has addressed 1,500 audiences in all 50 states and 8 foreign countries. An award-winning columnist for *Today's Christian Woman,* Liz is also the author of more than two dozen books, including her nonfiction bestseller, *Bad Girls of the Bible,* and her fiction bestseller, *Thorn in My Heart.*

ACKNOWLEDGMENTS

I write fiction, and the thought of writing something in the nonfiction realm was completely foreign to me. Oh, I'd entertained the thought a time or two: a cookbook, or perhaps a book describing my plotting and writing techniques. In the back of my mind I entertained the thought of sharing some of the lessons I'd learned along my spiritual journey, but I assumed that would be years down the road, when I'd semi-retired.

A phone call from Wendy Lawton changed everything. Wendy was a friend long before she became my agent. We'd attended a number of writing conferences together, and she'd heard me speak. My nonfiction book, she claimed, was already written. I didn't quite believe her, but I was willing to hear her out. Wendy suggested I print out the speeches I've given, articles I've written, and devotions I've shared. More than seven hundred pages spewed from my printer. My friend was right. The book was there all along, and that was how *Knit Together: Discover God's Pattern for Your Life* came into being.

I need to mention several others who have shaped and enlightened me on this spiritual journey. Marilyn Kimmel and Jackie Watson were the two neighbors who took me under their wing and brought me to Bible Study Fellowship. It's there that I discovered Jesus Christ and asked Him to be my personal Savior.

Kevin Hestead of First Christian Church in Port Orchard has been my pastor for twenty years. Kevin and his wife, Marcia, have deeply enhanced and influenced my walk with Jesus.

Wonderful Christians Barb Dooley, Lillian Schauer, Betty Roper, Sandy O'Donnell, Susan Plunkett, Krysteen Seelen, Linda Nichols, and many others who have prayed for me and loved me. They are shining examples of what it means to be a friend and a sister in Christ.

I'm forever grateful to God for sending Wayne Macomber into my life. My husband's encouragement, unfailing support, and love have given me wings. My life has been blessed because of him.

Finally, Anne Goldsmith, Sara Horn, and everyone at FaithWords at Hachette Book Group USA have been a joy to work with. If this book blesses a single woman or shines the light on another God-given purpose, it is due to this incredible publishing team who believed I had something genuine to offer other women. I'm grateful for the opportunity.

Debbie Macomber

■ ■ ■ ■

1
CREATED FOR PURPOSE

■ ■ ■ ■

Many people have a wrong idea of what
constitutes true happiness. It is not
attained through self-gratification, but
through fidelity to a worthy purpose.
                                        HELEN KELLER

Before you were born, before you knew the
world and the world knew you, there was
only One, the Creator, who knew you in
your most basic form. Even then, He had a
relationship with you. Growing within the
quiet shadows of your mother's womb,
blocked from even her eyes, God watched
you, marveling as your fingernails formed,
and your eyelashes fluttered, and the tiny
corners of your mouth turned up in pleasure
as you discovered your miniature thumb for
the very first time. You were His design, His
pattern, and you were beautiful to Him.

From the moment each of us is created,

23

God has a purpose for us. We don't necessarily know what it looks like at first, but we can be sure it's there, somewhere inside us. For a long time, I wondered what my purpose was. I knew I loved being a mother, and I knew I loved writing — but a writing career seemed to be something achievable only in my dreams, certainly not in real life for a twenty-nine-year-old housewife and mother of four.

When I think about what it means to be created by God for a purpose, my thoughts turn to Psalm 139. It is one of my favorite passages of the Bible because it combines two of my favorite things — knitting and the understanding of God's call on my life. We were knit together in our mothers' wombs (Psalm 139:13). We have been searched and known by the greatest designer in the universe (Psalm 139:1). We were designed for something special. I believe that something special is reflected in the strong desires God puts in our hearts through our dreams, through our passions, and through the things that bring us joy. It's through those things that we can discover what our purpose is, when we see for ourselves the pattern He's made for us and the dreams He's knitted together for us to live out.

I hope you'll go on an amazing adventure with me as we examine Psalm 139 in depth and discover the pattern God has for each of us when it comes to our purpose, our achievements, and so many other pieces that make up this fitted and well-worn garment we call life.

FINDING PURPOSE IN HUMBLE BEGINNINGS

Twenty-five years ago, I could not have imagined myself writing a book about realizing your dreams. I'm sure no one else could have imagined my writing one, either! I come from humble beginnings. I'm incredibly proud of my heritage and consider myself blessed in a number of ways because of my family. All four of my grandparents were German-speaking Russian immigrants. My father didn't graduate from high school and while my mother did, she had to move off the farm into town and work in order to obtain her education. Both of my grandfathers pushed a plow. There's absolutely nothing in my background that qualifies me to be a writer.

I got married out of high school to Wayne Macomber, and between 1970 and 1975 we had four children. I remember what my mother told me shortly after Dale, our youngest, was born. I hadn't slept an entire night in months; I was physically and mentally worn to a frazzle. A look of such joy came over my mother as she watched me with our newborn son. She smiled and said, "Debbie, these will be the happiest days of your life." I stared back at her in utter horror. "Mom, you mean to tell me it gets worse?" She laughed, promising me that one day I would treasure these days with my little ones. And she was right.

So I was the mom of four youngsters living on a limited income with nothing more than a high school degree, and on top of that, I'm dyslexic. School was always difficult for me, and I never managed to achieve anything higher than average grades. A scholarship or the possibility of college was never an option. At the time I didn't know I was dyslexic. The teachers didn't have a word for it then. I didn't know my troubles in school stemmed from a learning disability until my own children were diagnosed with dyslexia many years later. Dyslexia doesn't go away, so to this very day I'm a slow, thoughtful reader and a creative speller.

As a child of the fifties growing up in Yakima, Washington, words were both my passion and my torment. My mom said that from the time I was four years old, I went to sleep every night with a book in my hands. I loved visiting the local library where Beverly Bunn, the children's librarian, would read to us for story hour. She later married and went on to write novels, too. You may have read her work. Her married name is Beverly Cleary. I didn't know it at the time, but she had problems reading as a kid, too.

Despite my love for stories and for reading, I struggled in school. I was the only girl in my first-grade class to be in the Robin Reading Group, the lowest level there was. I can still remember sitting with my mother for a parent-teacher conference with my third-grade teacher. "Debbie is such a nice little girl, but she'll never do well in school," my mother was told. Whether it was a self-fulfilling prophecy, I don't know, but the teacher was right — I never did achieve high grades and remained an average student, so average, in fact, that academically I ranked fortieth in my graduating class of eighty girls.

The biggest complaint teachers had about me growing up was that I daydreamed. It was true. As early as I can remember, I liked creating stories, often when I was supposed to be paying attention in class. Storytelling actually became my niche when I was twelve or thirteen. I used to make up stories about the kids I babysat, entertaining them with silly names like Snickelfritz and Stinkyfoot, and they loved it — so much that their parents would pay me a dollar an hour when the going rate was just a quarter. A friend of mine likes to joke that even then, I was set on being successful! Maybe I was, but I certainly didn't know it.

Though reading was difficult, I persisted with it, and by the time I was in fifth grade, I had caught up with my classmates. I was ten when I started thinking about what it would be like to be a writer, and I wrote my first book the following year. I still remember the characters — the story was about triplets named Faith, Hope, and Charity, a precursor I'm sure to what have become my three angels — Shirley, Goodness, and Mercy — favorite characters of several Christmas books I've written over the years. I never told my teachers or friends I wanted to write because I was afraid they would tell me all the reasons it was impossible for me to be a writer. I didn't get good grades in English (or anything else), and my spelling was atrocious. I couldn't bear to have such a fragile dream trampled upon.

I am absolutely convinced that each of us is created with a God-given purpose. It's what I like to call the focus of our lives — the "what" that my life, and yours, is all about. Some people seem to know what their purpose is early on; they get up every morning with this innate passion for something; they walk around with fire in their bellies — a desire that doesn't go away. They have vision and determination, and they are ready to see all their dreams come true! For others, though, their purpose, their life's focus, seems much dimmer, harder to see. But that doesn't mean it isn't there.

If you've picked up this book, chances are you're trying to figure out what your purpose is or how to achieve that seemingly unreachable dream. Maybe you thought you knew what you wanted to do, but life's circumstances have left you wondering. Maybe you've never known. Or perhaps you do know, but, as I was, you're afraid. You're scared of what other people will think, or you fear that you'll fail. So you stick your purpose up on a shelf, thinking that maybe someday you'll get to it.

In the late seventies, my purpose, my focus to be a writer, was way, way out of reach and coated with a thick layer of dusty childhood doubts and the busyness of being a mother to four very active children. But every once in a while, in my mind, I'd take my purpose down and look at it, turn it around and wistfully think, *Maybe after the kids are grown.* Then, back on the shelf it went. Out of sight, out of mind. Almost. Until David got sick.

My cousin David Adler and I grew up together. We attended the same schools, lived in the same neighborhood, and worshipped at the same church. The only dates I got in high school were due to David. In fact, it was David, another cousin, Doug, and my brother Terry who made copies of my eighth-grade diary and sold them to the boys in my class. At the time, I was mortified, but the years have a way of changing one's perspective. These days, what I remember most is how many copies were bought!

As a young adult, David was diagnosed with leukemia. When he was admitted to Fred Hutchinson Cancer Research Center in Seattle, my husband, Wayne, and I were the closest family to the hospital, living just a few miles south of town. Although I didn't venture into the big city very often, I was determined to be with David, his wife, Rachel, and their daughter. From the day he arrived in Seattle from Yakima, I spent part of every day with my cousin. I was certain God would perform a miracle. I was convinced that God would heal him.

At the time, I hadn't been a Christian long. I was raised Catholic and attended the local parochial school for all twelve grades. In my parents' house there had always been a coffee-table Bible, but I never saw it open. Every Sunday when I went to Mass, I heard the four Gospels and the Epistles, but they never connected. Maybe I was too young to really care back then. I knew about God, but the God I grew up with was stern and vengeful. I didn't have a relationship with Him. I didn't know Him. I didn't realize Christ was my personal Savior; I knew only that my sins had nailed Him to the cross.

But at the age of twenty-two, after Wayne and I had married and I was a mother twice over, we moved to Seahurst, near Seattle. With two small babies born a year apart on my hips, I was invited to Bible Study Fellowship (BSF) by my neighbor Marilyn Kimmel. Until that point I'd never set foot inside a Protestant church, but I was hungry for friendship and so I went. I had the most uncomfortable feeling as soon as I got there. I was afraid if my parents ever found out what I was doing, they'd be upset. Then the teaching leader, Denise Adler, introduced herself. Adler is my maiden name, and it was as if God was saying to me that it was fine for me to be in these unfamiliar surroundings; I was home and this was family.

That week the class was studying the first four chapters of Nehemiah. I remember Marilyn telling me somewhat apologetically that this was the year BSF was studying the Minor Prophets. I told myself that was okay since I didn't know what a major one was. Surrounded by those dear ladies, as I got into the Word, it latched onto my heart. It wasn't long before I felt God tugging at me. I wanted the same relationship with Christ that my friends had. As I studied His Word, I surrendered my life to Jesus Christ and have never regretted that decision.

That's why, seven years later, because of that wonderful relationship I had with Jesus, I was absolutely convinced that God would heal my cousin David. After all, I knew my life had changed for the better, and I knew God could make a difference in David's life. And this was no mustard-seed faith; the faith I carried around was the size of avocados! I told David, "God is going to heal you. Through the love of Jesus Christ, you're going to be healed."

Knit Together for Purpose

"Whether I am knitting for myself or someone else, my passion for knitting enables me to express my creativity and produces a feeling of accomplishment." — Rita E. Greenfeder, Editor, *Knit 'N Style*

If you've ever read any of my books, you probably already know that I'm a big knitter. I started knitting as a twelve-year-old girl. My mother wasn't a knitter, and in fact, I didn't know a single person who knew how to knit. I pestered her until she took me to the local yarn store. The wonderful ladies there took me under their wing and taught me, and I've never been the same since. I knitted all through my school years until Wayne and I married, and then again periodically while the kids were growing up. But it was when I became a grandmother for the first time that the bug really took hold. I love to knit! I also love collecting yarn. In fact, I need an entire room to hold my yarn stash. It's difficult for me to resist stopping in a yarn store, no matter how many projects are already waiting for me at home. But knitting can often be a slow process. From start to finish, it takes time to complete. Knitting certainly requires patience and persistence. I find it's the same with finding your purpose.

But despite all my prayers and absolute certainty, David passed away on September 23, 1978. And suddenly, I didn't know what to believe. I was in a crisis of faith. I couldn't sleep; I couldn't pray. I couldn't read my Bible. I felt that God had let me down.

My questions ended one morning, though, when I tried to have devotions with the children. My son Ted was particularly antsy that day, and, exasperated, I tried again to get him to pay attention.

"Ted," I asked, for the twentieth time, "what do you have to do to get to heaven?"

He looked at me as if I had just asked what he'd had for breakfast.

"Die," he said.

His answer took a moment to sink in. But I realized he was right. David had died, but before his death he had come to know the same Jesus I did. Because he had accepted Christ, I had the assurance that David was in heaven. Furthermore, by the grace of God, David really had been healed.

That revelation was quickly followed by another: I could no longer afford to dream of being a writer *someday.* I could no longer stuff my dreams into the future with a long list of justifications. Life holds no guarantees. I realized then that it was time for me to move my life purpose forward. It was time to go after my dream.

Since we didn't have the money to buy a typewriter, we rented one. I placed that typewriter on the kitchen table and moved it at mealtimes. Every morning when the kids left for school, I moved the typewriter back to the table and wrote until they came home. I didn't have a lot of life experience at that point, but I knew I could write something with a happy ending. And after four kids, I needed one.

THE PASSION IN YOUR PURPOSE

I imagine that you're asking how I knew my purpose was to be a writer. Well, I didn't at first, not completely. But as I said earlier, I believe that God puts desires in our hearts through our dreams, through our passions, and through what brings us joy. When we can look through all of those things, we can find our purpose as we discover the customized blueprint, the pattern, God's made for each of us.

So, let's take a look at the passion in our purpose. Ask yourself these questions: *What is it that gets me excited? What do I love to do?*

I believe that what you enjoyed as a child often provides hints of what you should be doing as an adult. When I was young, I loved to read and tell stories. Maybe you loved to dress up your dolls, creating elaborate new fashions. Maybe you liked drawing. Or maybe you thrived on helping other people, or taking care of the neighbor's dog. Perhaps you enjoyed playing school or house, or caring for sick stuffed animals. Whatever you enjoyed most can give you clues to the purpose God has for you. As Rick Warren puts it so directly on the first page of *The Purpose-Driven Life,* "It's not about you."

God has a plan for your life and a purpose that fits into His master plan. But He doesn't want you to float through life waiting for a giant bolt of lightning to fall from heaven and point out what you're supposed to be doing. He gave each of us a brain as well as a heart. We have to listen to both to truly discover the pattern God has for our lives.

Unfortunately, when we talk about passion and purpose, we sometimes mistakenly equate anything we're passionate about to what we're supposed to be doing. Passion does not necessarily equal a calling to what your purpose or your dreams should be focused on. My husband is passionate about the Seattle Seahawks. We actually had season tickets for more than twenty-five years. Yet that doesn't mean he has the talent to go play football. I love collecting cameos, and I buy a new one every year. I treasure my cameo collection, but that doesn't mean I'm supposed to open a jewelry store or seek out seashells for the artisan to carve.

You can be passionate about a lot of things, but not everything you're enthusiastic about is necessarily what you're supposed to be doing. You need to watch only one episode of those auditioning for *American Idol* to understand that. Many of the people who step before the judges *desperately* want to sing. They *love* music, they *breathe* music, but they're so bad at it, they make the rest of us cringe and plug our ears!

When you are truly passionate about something that God has designed for you to do, things unexplainably click. You experience a profound sense of joy in what you do. It feels natural and it completes you. That's the way writing is for me. There are a lot of other writers out there who talk about how hard it is to actually sit down and write. Something always gets in the way. It's not that way for me — I love to write. I enjoy everything about the process of writing — the plotting, even revisions. When the time comes for me to sit down and pen the story, I'm so passionate about it, I can barely stand still. In my heart, I know this book is going to make a difference, a difference in my life and the lives of my readers.

Another great thing about passion is that it is contagious. Have you ever noticed how people are irresistibly drawn to someone with a lot of enthusiasm? Passion doesn't just set your own footsteps on fire; it can also spur and motivate others.

I remember so well those early days when I first decided to write. I was happy — happier than I could ever remember being in my life. I was so in love with the story and the words that I felt the need to stop and pinch myself to make sure this wasn't a fantasy or that I'd wake up and discover this was a dream. I could hardly wait to start work each day, and it's like that even now. The passion was there along with the purpose. This of course doesn't mean that every day is like a trip to Disneyland — passion shouldn't always be equated with fun. But if what you're doing doesn't spur you to experience joy or a sense of accomplishment, or provoke something inside you that makes you want to keep going, it's time to take a step back and reexamine what you're doing and whether the purpose you're pursuing is really the purpose God has in mind.

In his autobiography, C. S. Lewis writes about true joy and describes it as an "inconsolable longing."[1] Inconsolable. Unquenchable. An insatiable need to do what drives us, what God has put within each of us to carry out.

But understanding what fills us with passion is just one part of purpose. What happens when we don't feel any passion at all?

CREATED FOR PURPOSE — AND FLEXIBILITY

It's one thing to already be passionate; it's another to flounder around, trying to find something that captures our interests. You might feel afraid or uncertain or overwhelmed. My friend Joanne Hrycak lost her husband when the World Trade Center towers collapsed on 9/11. I know others who have lost their spouses to death or divorce, who now wonder what they're supposed to do with their lives. Where do they go from here? I also know women who dedicated their energy and time and focus to their children for years, and now that they're grown with lives of their own, these women wonder what's left for them. Are their lives over?

Let me assure you — your purpose does not end with your spouse or your children. God has so much more in store for you! Just look at what He says in His Word:

> For it is God who works in you to will and to act according to his good purpose. (PHILIPPIANS 2:13 NIV)

> And we know that in all things God works for the good of those who love him, who have been called according to his purpose. (ROMANS 8:28 NIV)

Oliver Wendell Holmes once stated that "most of us go to our graves with our music still inside us." The key is to find our music. We must be willing to be flexible when we start looking at our purpose and what makes us passionate.

Years ago I read a wonderful success story about a woman who longed to be on Broadway. It was her dream; she knew she was supposed to be on the big stage. So she packed up, moved to New York, and, like most aspiring actors and actresses, she struggled. The auditions were few and far between, and the successful auditions were even fewer. As time passed and no big roles came along, her dream became dimmer and dimmer. To make ends meet, she found a job with a limo company as a limousine driver. One day, she happened to pick up Liza Minnelli, an experienced Broadway performer in her own right. The young woman and Liza had a pleasant chat during the ride and discovered that they had quite a few mutual friends. Soon, Liza was requesting the young limo driver every time she needed a ride.

"You know, you should think about starting your own company," Liza told her new friend one day. Taking her suggestion seriously, the girl bought her own limousine on her credit card and started her own limo service. She now has one of the most successful limousine services in New York City, catering to the Broadway stars as well as other famous clientele. Her dream of working on Broadway was realized, but only after understanding that her original dream to work onstage needed modifying. Her audience changed. No, she wasn't performing to thousands in a theater; instead, she was performing for important clients, delivering not lines but incredible customer service. She learned that she had to be flexible as she sought out her purpose, her dream. She had to be willing to explore new roads, new avenues she hadn't thought about before.

Think about your own flexibility. How bendable are you when it comes to what you're passionate about? Remember what I said earlier about how it's important to use both your head and your heart when it comes to discovering God's pattern for your life? This is where the head part comes in.

What's Your P-Word?

If you have a one-track mind when it comes to your purpose, or if you struggle with even coming up with something to be passionate about, I hope you'll try this little experiment with me: Get out a clean sheet of paper and think of a word or a phrase that describes something that excites you or something you enjoy. Maybe it's books. Or music. Or ministry. Make it as general or as specific as you like. This is your core P-Word (*purpose* or *passion* — take your pick). Circle the word. Then think of as many other words as possible that relate to your P-Word, and draw lines like branches from

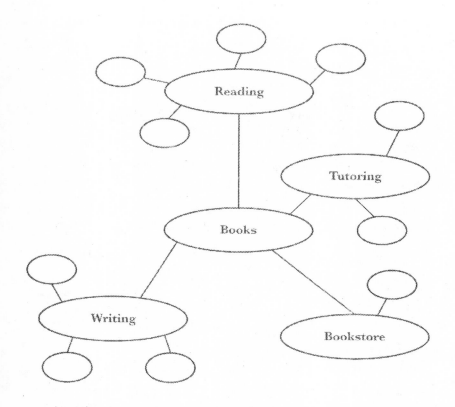

your P-Word to these other words, which we'll call your S-Words (*solution* words).

For example, if your P-Word is books, some of your S-Words could be tutoring, bookstore, writing, and reading. Once you brainstorm as many S-Words as possible, circle each of those and start over, treating each S-Word as a P-Word, until you have a number of ideas of jobs and activities you could do that involve that core passion or purpose you love. Now pick something that looks interesting and fun. Do some research to see what you can do with it! As you step out toward your purpose, you will begin to discover what God can do with you.

LIVING WITH PURPOSE

Purpose is not just a word we use when we talk about what God wants us to do with the life He's given us. It can also be a call to action. We were created for *purpose.* To be intentional. To move. To focus our actions and our abilities for a specific reason. When I set out to knit something for one of my children or grandkids, I usually let whomever I'm knitting for pick out the pattern and the yarn. That way I know I'm knitting something they'll like. When I take my grandkids along to the yarn store, I let them pick out the color and the buttons. Each design is purposely determined.

As much as we are called *for* a particular purpose, we are also called to live *with* purpose. Unfortunately, many of us fall short of this. Instead of living with clear purpose, we live in self-inflicted murkiness. We allow situations and people and everything in between to slow us down and keep us living in the clouds instead of the clear, bright sunshine of where God wants us to be.

Some of you may be thinking, *If only I can*

achieve this, or accomplish that, then life will be good. But your purpose doesn't end with that first step. It is an ongoing journey, and it requires a few different pieces of luggage.

Our purpose, or the focus of our lives, is the sturdy suitcase we never want to leave home without. This is the bag in which we carry everything we need for our journey. The basic essentials that are going to keep us looking clean and put together. When it comes to our focus, we want to make sure we don't leave those basics — like our goals, our determination, and our persistence — behind. When we're talking about purpose, all of these things are important, especially setting goals.

A few years ago, I was clearing out a drawer and found a tablet I'd written on in 1992. I'd been listening to a motivational tape, and the tape had suggested writing down five goals that seemed completely and totally out of reach. We were asked to exercise our goal-setting muscles, to imagine the seemingly impossible. My list consisted of: (1) consistent placement on the *New York Times* best-seller list; (2) books sold in audio format; (3) author tours; (4) movie deals; and (5) ABA (American Booksellers Association, now known as Book Expo America) appearances. At the time, these were impossible goals for someone writing category romance novels. But when I saw that list so many years later, I was stunned — *every single goal* on that piece of paper had come to pass. My basic luggage had never left my side.

If purpose is our suitcase, then passion is our carry-on. This is what keeps us excited and looking forward to our destination. Maybe it's a book or a travel guide or our favorite snack for the plane. Or maybe when it comes to our passion, it's what gets us excited, what helps us feel alive. It's the reason we do what we do; it's the people we want to help or the change we want to bring about.

The last piece required for the journey is patience. Think of it as your garment bag. It's as essential as passion and focus, but I think it's also the hardest. It's bulky and sometimes hard to carry, but it is such a necessary part of the trip.

After more than five years of constant rejections, I did finally reach my goal and sold my first book. Yet I wanted *more.* I wanted to sell more books; I wanted my name up there among the best sellers. I had climbed higher than I ever had before, and I really liked the view! No more bottom step for me! I wanted *more* success, and I wanted it *now.* Does that sound familiar?

I understand what it means to be impatient for your dream to take root and grow. Even though I knew from my own experience how important patience was, once I sold that first novel, I found myself in a competitive trap, walking faster and faster on a treadmill, comparing my career with others', wanting what they had. Eventually, I discovered the need for balance, for insight and emotional strength. I made it my goal to enjoy every step of the journey instead of being greedy for more and more.

In *My Utmost for His Highest,* Oswald Chambers writes about the importance of enjoying the journey:

> God's training is for now, not later. His purpose is for this very minute, not for sometime in the future. We have nothing to do with what will follow our obedience, and we are wrong to concern ourselves with it. What people call preparation, God sees as the goal itself.[2]

Be patient, trust in the journey, and worry less about the end goal. I sometimes joke that it took me only twenty years to become an overnight success, but it's really true. My dream didn't happen overnight for me, as you will discover in the next chapter, and it's unlikely that it will for you, either. But the most important thing is to learn and grow as an individual and as a child of God on the journey. And we must remember to always pack carefully.

The best piece of advice I can leave you with as we get ready to move from our purpose to our dreams is a passage from *The Message.* Galatians 6:1, 4–5 says:

Live creatively, friends. . . . Make a careful exploration of who you are and the work you have been given, and then sink yourself into that. Don't be impressed with yourself. Don't compare yourself with others. Each of you must take responsibility for doing the creative best you can with your own life.

It is my prayer for you that as you look to God for your purpose, you will continue along your journey by living creatively and with hope in the knowledge that God wants the best for you.

■ ■ ■ ■

2

CREATED FOR DREAMS

■ ■ ■ ■

Before a word is on my tongue
you know it completely, O LORD.

PSALM 139:4 NIV

To accomplish great things, we must not only act, but also dream; not only plan, but also believe.

ANATOLE FRANCE

From the time I was in junior high, I've kept a diary. I still have the one I kept through my high school years and all the years since, although now that I'm more mature and sophisticated, I refer to them as journals.

Sometime ago I was unpacking a box and came upon my journal from 1978. It was a spiral-bound notebook, and the wire had been twisted and bent out of shape, no doubt by one of my children. I remember 1978 well. My daughters, Jody and Jenny, had just started third and second grades, Ted was in kindergarten and Dale in preschool, and all four of the kids were involved in sports, music, Scouts, and dance classes.

The entire family was actively involved in our church.

The first page of that journal read:

January 1, 1978
Since the greatest desire of my heart is to somehow . . . some way, publish a book, I'll start by writing in the pages of this journal. . . .

As I read those words so many years later, a chill raced up and down my spine. I remembered what it was like to give my dream to the Lord. Getting published seemed impossible at the time, and yet, the dream persisted. By the time I discovered that journal, I had written dozens upon dozens of books that have been translated and published around the world.

God created us to dream. In Psalm 139:17–18, we read how precious God's thoughts are, and in fact, so vast in amount that they outnumber grains of sand. I believe those thoughts can translate into the dreams God gives each of us. He is the One who plants the dreams in our hearts; He is the One who gives them to us so we can be confident that He knows what our dreams are.

We were created to dream. Some of us

Knitting for Dreams

"When individual fibers are knitted together with a thread of emotion, they become an original, personal design. This creative process is my joyful obsession." — Emily Myles, Fibre Artist

To me, dreams are like the skeins of yarn I have in my yarn room. All of those wonderful colors and textures are just waiting to be pulled off the shelf and knit into something beautiful. You never know what wonderful creations a knit pattern or a dream can become.

Sometimes when I'm getting ready to start a new knitting project, I'll see a specialty yarn and I'll think, *Oh, wouldn't that be cute around the sleeves or the yoke?* It's so easy to add little embellishments to a basic pattern.

In fact, that reminds me of a pattern I'm working on right now that I found in a knitting magazine. It's a shawl that's knitted on the diagonal, with plain colors and plain yarn. The other day I was in the yarn store, and I saw a beautiful shawl hanging up, on display. Every panel was a different color and yarn type, and it was absolutely gorgeous. When I asked about it, the lady at the store said, "You won't believe where I got the pattern." It was the exact pattern I was working on at the time, only she had used different yarns, different colors, and different textures. What had been plain and ordinary was now stunning.

That's what happens when we use the imagination God has given us. That's what dreaming is all about.

dream of exotic once-in-a-lifetime trips or a bigger house or a certain car. Some of us dream of repairing a broken relationship or regaining our health. We dream for our families, for our children, for ourselves. We dream of doing incredible things; we dream of simpler times. We dream of having the perfect job — and some of us dream of not needing a job at all. We dream of the knight on the white steed coming to our rescue. We dream of obtaining the means and the resources to help others.

There's an old story from mythology that tells about the ancient Greeks back when the earth was young. According to the myth, the gods on Mount Olympus created the earth, man, and all the beasts. Once they'd finished creating all living things, they had one thing left to do, and that was to hide the secret of life where it wouldn't be found until man had grown in consciousness to the point that he was ready to receive it.

The gods argued back and forth about where this precious secret should be hidden. One suggested the highest mountain, certain that man wouldn't search for it there. But another god countered that man, with his insatiable curiosity and ambition, would eventually climb even the highest of peaks. The next idea was to hide the secret of life at the bottom of the deepest ocean. But that, too, was dismissed. Man was created with boundless imagination and a burning desire to explore the world — sooner or later, he would find a means of reaching even the deepest oceans.

Finally, one of the gods offered this solution: "Let us hide this secret in the last place man will ever look. A place that he will come to only when he has exhausted all other possibilities."

"And where is that?" asked the other gods.

"We will hide it in the human heart."

I believe that the secret of life this story refers to is the unspoken dreams each of us keeps hidden inside. It's our covered-up aspirations, our buried longings, the wordless wonders we hold so deep within ourselves, contained inside our hearts.

Unspoken Dreams

For me, writing was the ultimate dream, but for many years, it was an unspoken dream. It was a secret hope I had hidden away for most of my childhood. I didn't receive a lot of encouragement from my parents; in fact, they probably never even realized how badly I wanted to write. My parents were very busy, active, popular people. My mother worked as a waitress, and my father had his own upholstery company, so my brother and I were raised by babysitters. Writing was an incredible, beautiful dream, but it was also very scary because I was afraid it couldn't happen for someone like me — someone who had struggled in school, who had never done well academically despite my best efforts. How could I ever hope to publish a book?

For years, I kept that dream a secret known only to me, until my senior year in high school when the principal, Sister Anna

Maureen, called me into her office. It was traditional for Sister to ask a question of each student of the graduating class of St. Joseph Academy.

"Debbie, what do you want to do after graduation?"

"I am going to write books," I told her. Once the words were out of my mouth I immediately burst into tears. Dear Sister Anna Maureen patted me on the back, called my mother, and promptly sent me home. She must have thought I was having an emotional breakdown. You see, that was the first time I'd ever uttered those words out loud; the first time I'd allowed that whisper of a sentence repeated over and over in my mind and in my heart to actually leave my lips.

There's a difference between secret dreams and spoken dreams. Remember riding the seesaw at school when you were a kid? As long as you had your feet on the ground, you had control of that seesaw. But the moment you lifted your feet off the ground, or even better, used your feet to push yourself off, you were airborne. You were at the mercy of gravity and your friend on the other side. Secret dreams are safe; they're yours alone, and they let you stay close to the ground where it's comfortable and secure. But when you let a dream go airborne, when you say it out loud to a friend or even to yourself, that dream becomes more tangible, more real, and even a bit more dangerous.

You put yourself out there, hanging in a sense, when you speak your dreams out loud, because you now have a choice. You can do something with that dream, or you can let it lie there. We're going to talk about risk in more detail in the next chapter, but spoken dreams are risky because you've given them a place on the seesaw. They can go airborne or they can land with a thud. They can also get stuck. Ever have a friend who outweighs you sit on the other end of the seesaw and refuse to get up? Then you know what I'm talking about!

God gives us our dreams for a reason. He wants us to use them for His glory and for His good. But we won't be able to do that if we never allow our secret dreams to become spoken ones.

What is your biggest dream? What is the thing that most hangs on your heart and your mind? Say it out loud: "I want to . . ."

Don't think about the obstacles or the silliness of it or the small chance you think it has of coming to be — just say it out loud. Wipe the tears away if they come. Now, get ready to do something about it.

Dream with Determination

I believe there are two different types of dreams we each experience: everyday whimsical dreams and daily determined dreams. Everyday whimsical dreams are dreams that don't stick. They flit in and out of our thoughts and feelings, but they lack the passion, the purpose, and the drive to stay around for a while.

Determined dreams are a different story. These are the dreams that go places. These are the dreams that keep us awake at night, that get us up in the morning and ready to go for it all over again. These are the dreams God gives us that support our purpose, that create the direction we set our life's course to.

These dreams, however, don't succeed without work and planning. That's why it's so important to chart your dreams. Just like a captain of a ship long ago used to set his course by charting the stars in the sky, so we, too, must chart our dreams.

We will talk about goal planning in a later chapter, but the most important thing you can do is to map out the dream to see where it can take you. This can be enormously helpful because either it will give you the road map to succeed in your dream and help define your purpose, or it will show you the washed-out bridges and dead-end roads that will make it impossible, and alert you that it's time to rethink your dream. It takes time, and it is not nearly as much fun to plan out your dream as it is to wistfully think about your dream, but it's so important if you truly want to succeed.

So let's think about your dream. What is it you want to do most? Do you want to open a business? To become a performer — a musician or an actress? Do you want to work with your hands in the medical field, or work with your hands as an artist? Whatever it is, it's time to sit down and give it an honest evaluation so you can plot your dream's course.

Look at a map of the United States. Let's say that your dream starts in Los Angeles and your goal is to get to New York City. Or maybe you'll start in Seattle and make your way to Orlando, Florida. Wherever you start, you need to know where you're headed, and, beyond that, you need to know how you will get there.

When you plan a cross-country trip, you need to account for stops along the way, possible delays, rush-hour traffic, and even construction detours. It's the same with your dream. Ask yourself these questions:

- What will it take to achieve my dream? What are the major steps that will be required?
- What can I do to save? Are there financial goals I need to set? Realistically, how long will it take to reach those goals? What can be done to speed up the process?
- Do I need any special education? Do I need to take classes or can I read books on the subject?
- Do I need any special equipment? If so, where will I get it, and how much will it cost?
- Whom can I go to for advice about my dream? Whom can I trust to give wise counsel?
- What are some of the roadblocks I may encounter? What are some possible ways I can get through these?
- How long do I think it will take to achieve my dream? What can I do to keep going when it gets hard? At what point should I stop?

Once you've sat down and answered each of these questions honestly, you will have a good indication of whether your dream is truly achievable. And that brings us to the next point. If your dream hits a brick wall, does that really mean it's over? Not necessarily.

No Admittance

The first time I visited my cousin David in the hospital, I somehow ended up in Swedish Hospital instead of Fred Hutchinson Cancer Research Center, which was where David was being treated. I knew the hospitals were connected by a sky bridge, but try as I might, I couldn't find it. I wandered down corridor after corridor, but after several attempts, I realized I was hopelessly lost. In frustration, I stopped a physician and asked if he could tell me the way.

"It's simple," he assured me. "All you need to do is walk down this hallway, take the first right, and walk through the door marked 'Absolutely No Admittance.' "

When I think about those directions now, I have to smile because I realize that experience is what gave me courage to walk through other doors that seemed far beyond my capabilities. One lesson I've learned is that God often met me at that door marked "Absolutely No Admittance" and held it open for me. I'm here to tell you, He can do the same for you. But you have to be willing to walk through the hard places to enjoy the reward.

After I had written for about two years with only rejections to show for all that effort, my husband, Wayne, came to me one day with a sad look on his face.

"Honey, I'm sorry, but we just aren't making it financially. I need you to find a job."

It was early 1980, and Wayne stood in the kitchen doorway, clutching a handful of bills. My stomach clenched, and I swallowed an automatic protest before I saw the look of regret in his eyes. I knew it was hard for Wayne to ask me to seek employment, but I also knew we were going deeper into debt each month while I struggled to sell my first novel. I thought about how hard I had worked since David's death, when I came to the realization that life doesn't offer any guarantees. I wasn't politely tapping against the door of opportunity — I'd thrown the full force of my determination into it! And despite the rejections and the times I wondered whether I had the talent or grit to get there, I kept going. Over and over I rammed my soft-shelled dream against an impenetrable wall of doubts.

But everything came crashing to a halt that Sunday afternoon when Wayne set down the unpaid bills in front of me.

Together we reviewed our finances, and I realized there wasn't any alternative. I had to get a job, one that would contribute to our family income instead of draining it.

So, with the newspaper in hand, I circled three positions to apply for the next morning. Because I'd married as a teenager, I didn't have any marketable job skills. Even if I was fortunate enough to get hired right away, I'd be lucky to receive anything above minimum wage.

As I looked up from the newspaper, my gaze fell on the typewriter, and I knew this would be the end of my hopes and dreams of ever selling a novel. All four of the children were involved in a variety of activities. There simply weren't enough hours in the day for me to keep up with their wacky schedules, work forty hours a week, maintain the house, and still write. I might as well kiss my dream good-bye.

A million doubts battered me from all sides as I circled those three job listings in the newspaper. There was a swing-shift opening at the local 7-Eleven. A dentist was looking for a receptionist. And the local cleaners wanted to hire a cashier. There was nothing wrong with any of these positions, and they were the only ones I qualified for, but I felt that I was born to write.

I remember going to bed that night and trying not to let Wayne know how depressed and miserable I was. In the darkness, with Wayne sleeping softly at my side, I recalled the joy and enthusiasm I'd experienced as I began this venture. Despite everything, I felt so sure God was leading me to write. I was willing to tackle every obstacle, every doubt. With my Bible and a copy of Norman Vincent Peale's *The Power of Positive Thinking* at my side, I was certain that sooner or later a New York publisher would recognize my talent and offer me a contract.

I had refused to give up, and yet here I was, two and a half years into the journey, and I hadn't sold a single word. Instead of contributing to our family income, I was draining our already meager finances. I just never believed it would end like this.

As hard as I tried, I couldn't sleep. In the darkness, I prayed and offered my dream back to God. He was the One who'd given it to me in the first place, and I'd gone as far with it as I humanly could. The rest was up to God. Perhaps someday I'd be able to write again. Perhaps . . .

About two or three in the morning, Wayne rolled over and whispered, "Are you awake?"

"I haven't been to sleep yet," I confessed.

He waited a moment and then asked, "What's wrong?"

My heart was so heavy that I blurted out the truth. "You know, I really think I could have made it as a writer."

Wayne didn't say anything for a long time. Then he sat up and turned on the light. An eternity passed before he said, "All right, honey, go for it. We'll make whatever sacrifices we need to make."

How fortunate I am to have a husband who has always been willing to believe in me.

I wish I could tell you it was only a matter of a few weeks before New York recognized my talent and offered me that first contract. But it was another two and a half years of budgeting difficulties and financial struggles before the sale of my first novel. Almost five years passed from the day we rented the typewriter until the long-awaited phone call from New York.

Those years of holding on to that dream taught me many valuable lessons. I believe God plants dreams in our hearts so we'll learn to turn to Him, to trust Him to see them to fruition.

"For I know the plans I have for you," declares the LORD, "plans to prosper you and not to harm you, plans to give you hope and a future." (JEREMIAH 29:11 NIV)

God wants the *best* for you — not the average and not the mundane. He wants your future to be full; He wants your gifts to be used! He wants to see you prosper and flourish as you use the skills and talents and gifts He has given you. But He doesn't just hand all of these wonderful dreams and successes to you on a heavenly platter — no, trust me, there will be plenty of ups and downs along the way! God uses those moments to draw you even closer to Him.

THE RAIN BEFORE THE SUNSHINE

In those first five years, I wrote four manuscripts, and each one was rejected. I used to tell people the rejections came so fast they hit me in the back of the head on the way home from the post office. After Wayne and I had our 2:00 a.m. talk and he showed his willingness to continue to support me in my dream, I realized I needed to do something to start contributing to our family's income. That's when I started selling a number of nonfiction articles.

In 1982, I sold an article and was paid $350 — more than I'd ever received. It was enough to pay my way to attend my first writers' conference put on by the Pacific Northwest Writers Association. The piece I sold was about my cousin David's death. Ironically, it was not just his death that spurred me into pursuing my dream; it was also his story that helped me get there.

Two editors from a major romance publisher were scheduled to attend this conference. Writers were invited to submit proposals to be reviewed by these editors before the conference. I still remember the day I received notification that my manuscript had been one of those chosen by the editors. A strange feeling came over me unlike anything I'd ever experienced before or since. In that moment I knew: I was going to sell that novel.

"I'm going to make it," I told my husband. "I'm really going to make it."

A month later, on the first day of the conference, I found myself crammed into a workshop with three hundred other women, all as eager and excited about selling their stories as I was. The two editors introduced themselves and then claimed that of the ten manuscripts they had reviewed, only one of them showed promise.

I knew it was mine. I was positive! It was a foregone conclusion. In my heart, I knew. After all, I'd invested nearly five years at this point and written four books all the way through. My story was more than good. It was great!

I'd rewritten *Heartsong* until it shone so brightly it was in danger of blinding an editor with the pure strength of my genius. Boy, did I have a cold wake-up call coming.

To put it mildly, my manuscript was not the one the editor liked. When she got to my story, she had the entire room laughing at the implausibility of my plot. By the time she finished her cutting critique, I was numb.

After the workshop was over, I swallowed my pride and quietly made my way over to the editor. I explained to her who I was and which story was mine. I accepted the importance of revision and wanted her to know I was willing to do whatever was necessary to make my story publishable.

I asked her if she would be willing to review my manuscript again if I rewrote the proposal. As long as I live, I'll never forget the look of pity that came into her eyes. She leaned forward, pressed her hand on my arm, and said, "Honey, throw it away."

Throw it away.

That proposal was as perfect as I could make it. It was the very best I was capable of writing, and after investing nearly five years of my life into writing, into pursuing my dream, someone thought I should throw it away, like worn-out shoes or a rusty bicycle.

That night, I returned home, dragging a whole lot more than my tail. These were hard times for the Macomber family. Wayne was living in Fairbanks, eating one meal a day, waiting for work on the Alaska pipeline.

Try as I might, I couldn't sleep. At about three in the morning, I sat alone in our living room and watched the shadows on the wall. They seemed to taunt me. "So you think you're going to be a writer. So you think you can make a career of this. So you think you can publish a book. This is what you get for dreaming. This is all that your dreams are worth. Five years, and the best you can do is 'throw it away.'"

My youngest son came downstairs a short while later. I gently told him it was much too early for him to be up and walked him back to his room. When I tried handing him his favorite yellow blanket, he calmly told me that at seven years old, he didn't need his blanket anymore.

I remember standing there in the shadows of our dark hallway outside his room and thinking that if he didn't need that security blanket, I did. I stretched back out on the

70

couch, wrapped that blanket over my legs, and sighed. If there was ever a time I needed to be positive, it was now. If there was ever a time to take comfort from my Bible, it was now.

I reached for my devotional and saw that the suggested reading for the day was John 14. I was in no mood to read an entire chapter, so I decided I would read the first verse and the last verse. The first verse said, "Let not your heart be troubled" (NKJV). I never realized what a joker God could be until then. I snickered and flipped the page to the last verse. It read, "Arise, let us go from here" (NKJV).

I went, all right. That morning, I headed straight back to that writers' conference and asked for a refund. They wouldn't give it to me.

So I went to a children's fiction workshop. Maybe I wasn't cut out for women's fiction. Since nearly every word I'd sold up to that point had been about my kids, maybe that was what I should be writing.

I remember very little about that workshop except one important piece of advice that helped me more than I ever would have thought possible. An author advised the group to never leave a rejected manuscript sitting on the desk. One editor's trash might be another publisher's treasure.

A few short weeks after the conference, I acted on that advice, and defiantly sent off a query letter to Silhouette Books, impatiently waiting for a reply. None came. One morning, I couldn't stand the wait any longer and decided to mail my manuscript off whether they wanted to see it or not.

DETERMINED DREAMS

Looking back on that day, I remember that the line at the Kent, Washington, post office had never felt longer. After piling my four children into our family station wagon, I stood awaiting my turn to hand over my manuscript. Along with the package went my fragile hopes, my dreams of ever succeeding as a writer — all the hope a single heart could hold.

It was a gamble, I'll admit. A big one. All I could do was pray that I was doing the right thing. The problem was, I couldn't bear to look at that manuscript sitting on the corner of my desk for another minute. It challenged me every time I passed, daring me to think of myself as a writer. All the ugly, negative voices of my childhood echoed through my mind. Finally, I couldn't take not knowing. That was when I decided I didn't care — I was mailing off my book.

I remember it cost ten dollars to mail off the completed manuscript: five dollars for postage and five for the return postage. I don't know if you can imagine how much ten dollars is to someone living on $150 a week.

As I stood there at the front of the line, praying that I was doing the right thing, the postal employee leaned forward and reached for the ten-dollar bill. "You have to let go of the money," he said. Reluctantly, I handed it to him, but as I did, a sick feeling came over me. It was out of my hands now, and all I could do was wait and hope and try to believe.

After we got home from the post office, one of my sons raced down to the mailbox to collect the mail. Inside was a letter from Silhouette Books in response to my query letter, an answer that I'd been too impatient to wait for. It read, "Do not send us your manuscript: we are not buying at this time."

My heart sank and I understood where that sick feeling had come from earlier. I had just wasted ten very precious dollars. I walked into the house, lay down on the couch, and didn't get up for the rest of the day. There was no way I could continue this madness. My fiction writing days were over.

Or so I thought.

Friends, I know what it's like to be told to throw your dream away. Some of you have been told to throw your dream away, too, and some of you actually believe that maybe those voices are right; maybe you aren't cut out for this dream, this pursuit, and this passion that propels you forward.

I'm here to tell you: don't listen.

I read about a study in which scientists took a set of guppies and a set of piranhas and put them in the same fish tank with only a slab of glass separating them. The piranhas, looking at a tasty meal, hit the glass over and over as they tried to get to the guppies. They stopped once they realized their attempts were hopeless. But then a curious thing happened. The scientists removed the glass and the piranhas still left the guppies alone. Even though the glass was gone, they had internalized their limitations and were no longer interested in pushing beyond the boundaries originally set for them.

The same thing happened with a group of jumping fleas. Scientists put a jar over the fleas and after bumping the top of the jar repeatedly, the fleas learned to jump much lower. Even after the jar was removed, the fleas continued to jump only as high as when the jar contained them. They allowed their environment to define how far they could go.

This is the way it can be with dreams. We let difficult circumstances, other people, and external forces hamper and dim our hopes. We allow these invisible barriers to keep us from soaring. I know how real those obstacles can seem when you're up against them, but I also believe it's all in your outlook. Do you believe God's given you a dream? Or do you believe the lies you're told that are disguised as genuine limitations?

So often when it comes to our dreams, our greatest enemy is ourselves. We are very good at making excuses, aren't we? Some of them are downright brilliant. Over the years, I've probably heard them all, and I've been guilty of making up more than a few of my own.

When you can see the lie for what it is, you can take the first step toward achieving your dreams. As the Bible says, the truth will set you free (John 8:32). Behind each of these lies we encounter, there's a truth we must face if we're going to move forward and achieve our dreams.

Lie #1: It's Who You Know

How often have you heard that success depends on knowing the right people? That you have to network in order to "net" work? I'm not saying that it doesn't help to get to know other people — or as Steven Chandler, a motivational speaker, says, it's what you do with whom and what you know that makes a difference. When I first started writing, I didn't know a single other writer. I didn't have an agent, and I didn't know the proper format in which to submit my work to a publisher, nor did I know how to get noticed. But that didn't keep me from trying!

Steven Chandler tells the story of how his first book, *100 Ways to Motivate Yourself,* was published. By profession, he's a motivational speaker, and at the end of his talks, he would hand out a sheet listing twenty-one ideas for self-motivation. For years, his friends told him he needed to put it in a book format, and so he started adding to his list until he'd reached a hundred different ways to get motivated. For years, the list sat on his desk, and then one summer his daughter needed money to go to camp and he quickly drafted up a book proposal and hired his daughter to type out the letters to go to the publishers.

With meticulous detail, his fourteen-year-old daughter typed each query letter and slipped it and a short proposal inside each envelope. She thought he had a great idea and she said so, but the whole time she was doing this, Steven Chandler thought, *The poor girl doesn't have a clue how difficult it is to publish a book.*

When he drove her to camp, there were sixty stamped manila envelopes in the backseat of his car. He almost didn't mail them because he didn't know a single person in New York. He didn't have an agent, and everyone knows you can't sell a book without an agent. Steven didn't want to disappoint his daughter, though, so he dropped the envelopes off at the post office and promptly forgot about the whole thing.

Three weeks later he had phone calls from *seven* publishers. Seven! He got so excited, he phoned his daughter at camp.

"Sweetheart, guess what? I've got seven publishers who are interested in buying my book. They all called me — can you believe it?"

His daughter's lack of response astounded him. "Stephanie, did you hear?"

"Yes, but, Dad, only seven?"

Steven Chandler didn't really believe he had a chance to sell his book, but he was willing to give it a shot in an effort to help his daughter earn money for camp — and in the process, he learned a valuable life lesson. It *isn't* who you know, and when we tell ourselves it *is,* we're lying to ourselves in order to discount our dreams. I think too often we rely on other people to make our dreams happen. But if it's not *their* dream, it's not *their* passion.

As a parent, no one knows your child better than you. It's the same with your dreams. No one knows your dreams better than you and your heavenly Father. It's up to you to take action and believe.

Lie #2: I'm Too Old

How often have you heard yourself or your friends say this? It's far too easy to use age as an excuse for almost anything. We're too old to try anything new, too old to do things we used to do as kids, too old to keep doing what we've been doing. We get ourselves in an age rut — we can't go backward, but we're unwilling to move forward.

A few years ago, I met an incredible woman who was in her eighties. Until just recently, Marilyn George was a commercial fisherman in Alaska. She decided to write about her experiences. I have rarely attended a more entertaining autographing.

She told of her hair-raising experiences while living aboard a fishing vessel and raising her children. As the story progressed, she dressed up in her fishing gear and told tale after tale of life in Alaska. Marilyn believes that age is a matter of the mind, and I have to agree with her.

I swim five mornings a week with a group of ladies all in their eighties. Looking at them, you'd be hard-pressed to believe their ages. They're full of energy, laughter, and enthusiasm. When I grow up, I want to be just like them.

For years, I've heard people say they have always wanted to be a writer, a musician, a poet, an actor, or any of a number of other things. My automatic response is always, "What's stopping you?" Their response is almost always the same, too. "I'm too old to start now." What all of us have to remember is that we are as old as we want to be.

Golda Meir was seventy-one when she became prime minister of Israel. George Bernard Shaw was ninety-four when one of his plays was first produced. Benjamin Franklin was a framer of the United States Constitution when he was eighty-one.[1]

Saying we're too old is one way of admitting that what we think we're too old to do is something that appeals to us, but we aren't willing to pay the price. It's an excuse, and all too often a convenient one. Don't let it be one of yours.

LIE #3: IT'S TOO HARD

One of the biggest obstacles to our dreams is our own line of thinking:

- I'll never make it.
- I can't do it.
- It's impossible. There's no way.

I call these kinds of thoughts negative self-thinking, and this kind of thinking has no place around our God-given dreams.

There are enough natural obstacles to success without creating new ones. There are plenty of hills that are hard enough to climb without adding weights to our dreams. That's what negative self-talk does. It weighs us down, sets up roadblocks, and defeats us even before we get out of the starting gate. This is the most lethal of all lies. If we're going to succeed, if we're going to see our dreams come true, we need to recognize this lie for what it is and refuse to listen.

I was shopping with a friend in New York who was struggling to lose weight. With every outfit she tried on, she said the same thing: "I am so fat; I am disgusting."

I finally had to stop her.

"Would you say that to me?" I asked her. "Would you say, 'Debbie, you look so fat, you're disgusting'?"

"Never!" she said, a horrified look on her face.

"Then why would you say it to yourself?"

That's negative self-talk, and if you say it often enough, you start to believe it.

For most of my life, I have struggled with my weight. For years, I wrote in my journal about being fat and weak; I had no willpower when it came to food. But three years ago I decided I was never going to say that again. I am a child of God, and I am strong because God makes me strong. He gives me the strength I need (Psalm 29:11; Isaiah 41:10). I'm never going to put negative thoughts about my weight in my head again.

We are our own worst judges, our own worst enemies. God loves us, and He would never say the things to us that we say to ourselves. So why do we say such ugly, negative things to ourselves? Why do we insist on being negative? I know a woman who makes it a point to never talk badly about her husband. Her view is that she chose him, she married him, and if there's something wrong with him, it's a reflection on her, not necessarily her husband. She can make the choice to enjoy the good in her husband, or she can choose to reflect only the bad. It's the same with our relationship with God. We denigrate His position of power and authority and good over everything, including our lives, when we denigrate ourselves. Just as God made Adam and Eve in the Garden and saw that they were good, so He made us! We are good in His eyes, and we need to remember that we are the pinnacle of His creation.

One of the best things you can do is to be aware of when you practice negative self-talk and immediately turn it around to a positive. "This dress may not look good on me, but another one will." "God has given me nice legs." We need to remember that we are fearfully and wonderfully made.

Actually, instead of talking to myself, I like to talk to God instead. It's difficult to complain to God about how terrible you are when you remember you're talking to the original designer. He loves you, and He wants only the best for you. And He views you as beautiful.

You know, even after getting that letter back from Silhouette Books telling me not to send my novel, deep down I knew I wasn't ready to give up. I still believed in the dream God had placed within me. In my heart of hearts, I knew I was supposed to be a writer. It was my dream, it was my passion, and I believed with all my heart it was my purpose. And just a couple of weeks after sending my manuscript off to the publisher and thinking I had wasted ten very precious dollars, I got *the* phone call.

It was September 29, 1982, at 4:39 p.m. When I answered the phone, it was Mary Clare Susan, an editor for Silhouette Books at Simon & Schuster. Mary Clare made me an offer on the book. The very same book the other editor had told me no amount of rewriting would even make sellable. The very same book another editor had told me to throw away. I believe I said a grand total of five words the entire conversation: *hello, yes, thank you,* and *good-bye.* The story ended up being the first Silhouette book ever reviewed in *Publishers Weekly,* a major periodical in the publishing world. Because of *Heartsong* I was pictured in *Newsweek.* All for a book an editor told me to throw away.

BELIEVE IN YOUR DREAMS

Friends, I know what it's like to believe in your dreams and at the same time experience the uncertainty that often goes with them. It can be wonderful and frightening at the same time; it can be exciting and it can be heart-wrenching. But God has a plan for you, and that includes your dreams.

We were created to dream, to imagine, and to wonder. By doing anything less, we rob God of the opportunity to make those dreams come true. Believe in your dream, and ask God to show you the open door to that dream. And if that door closes, ask Him to open another. I promise you, He will, but you must be willing to walk through the doors so often marked "Absolutely No Admission."

■ ■ ■ ■

3
CREATED FOR RISK

■ ■ ■ ■

You hem me in — behind and before; you
    have laid
your hand upon me.

PSALM 139:5 NIV

Unless there is an element of risk in our exploits for God, there is no need for faith.

HUDSON TAYLOR

When we step forward in our purpose and pursue our dreams, there is always an element of risk that accompanies our journey. Psalm 139:23 talks about asking God to test and know our thoughts. When we set out to follow God's plan for our lives, we are throwing our own plans to the wind. It's risky; it's scary. But it is so worthwhile because we know our Savior's hand holds us and God, our Creator, guides us. With risk grows trust, and just as we were created for purpose and for dreams, we were created for risk.

I am a case study in how to be an overnight success in twenty years or less. As I mentioned earlier, it took me years of franti-cally pounding against opportunity's door before I sold my first novel. What I discov-ered during that time was that anything worth pursuing has an element of risk to it. It's risky to pursue your dreams because while there's a chance you might succeed, there's a chance you might fail, too.

Lucinda Williams was one lady willing to take that chance. Originally from Missouri, Lucinda moved to Dallas, Texas, sometime in the mid-1800s. After she settled in, she asked her landlady if there was a Baptist church there that she could attend. The landlady's curt reply was that there wasn't, and she hoped there never would be. Lu-cinda discovered that people had tried to start a Baptist church three different times in the town's recent past, and all three at-tempts had met with failure. She knew the odds weren't stacked in her favor, but she decided to take the risk.

On July 20, 1868, Lucinda and ten oth-ers, including her husband, organized a Baptist church. They had no building, they had no money, and they had very little sup-port. During those first few years, it wasn't clear whether the church would make it or not. But Lucinda kept going. She started the church's Sunday school, she created the church's mission society, and five years later, she convinced the women of the church to give more than six hundred dollars to help the church accomplish its purpose, an enormous amount of money for that time period. Because Lucinda was a woman who saw her purpose clearly, because she was passionate about her dream and willing to risk everything for it, she was able to plant the seeds that began First Baptist Church of Dallas, Texas, a church that later went on to become one of the largest churches in the world.

In John 10:10, Jesus says, "I have come that they may have life, and that they may have it more abundantly" (NKJV). Not only has the Lord called us to be self-assured, strong women of faith, but that verse you just read makes it absolutely clear that He longs for each of us to experience life to the full. He yearns for us to taste, see, smell, touch — to grab hold of life with both hands and revel in it.

Too often, though, we settle for Hamburger Helper instead of filet mignon. We take the good instead of going for the great. We accept the minimum instead of asking for the maximum. Why do we do this? I think most of us can readily accept that God wants us to live life to the fullest — that sounds fabulous. But when it comes to talking about our gifts — our dreams — that's scary. We're afraid we'll be called on to do something with them, and once we head down that path, there's no turning back.

But that's the "abundantly" part God is talking about. When we are in His will, doing what He wants us to do, in His plan, we are living life and living it large!

CONQUERING OUR FEARS

It's normal to be fearful when we go into unknown territory or try something new. It's okay to be scared — but we can't let fear paralyze us. We can't let trepidation prevent us from succeeding in our dreams.

In his book *If You Want to Walk on Water, You've Got to Get Out of the Boat,* John Ortberg notes that fear is the subject of the most common single command in the whole Bible:

> There's a two word phrase listed in all sixty-six books of the Bible and that phrase is FEAR NOT. God doesn't want us to be afraid, He wants us to reach out and grab hold of life, the abundant life, with both hands and revel. In Psalm 38:4 He says, "Taste and see that the Lord is good."

90

This is His most frequently repeated instruction. He wants us to be strong and courageous. You can trust me. Fear not. Why does God command us not to fear? Fear doesn't seem like the most serious vice in the world. It never made the list of the Seven Deadly Sins. No one ever receives church discipline for being afraid. So why does God tell humans to stop being afraid more often than He tells them anything else? My hunch is that the reason God says "Fear Not" so often . . . [is] because fear is the number one reason we are tempted to avoid doing what God asks us to do.[1]

Many years ago I ran across 2 Timothy 1:7, which says, "For God has not given us a spirit of fear and timidity, but of power, love, and discipline" (NLT). This became my life verse — whenever I feel afraid, or doubtful, or unsure of something, I repeat this verse to myself. I read these words over and over. I internalize them and make them my own. Every time I sign an autograph, I list that verse beneath my name as a reminder to me and to others that with God nothing is impossible.

Fear not! God wants me to be a woman of faith, a woman of conviction, and He wants the same for you as well. He wants us to walk with our heads high — not weighed down by worry and fear with our eyes focused on the ground. He wants us to stand straight and tall, filled with confidence and poise, certain in the assurance that He is right there with us, walking with us as we take those risks on our journey by His design. He tells each one of us to stand up and be proud of who and what we are — and not to be afraid of using the talents He's given us.

THE ART OF RISK-TAKING

I enjoy reading business books on a fairly regular basis. One of the books that made a profound difference in my thinking about risk-taking and overcoming my fears of success and reaching my dreams was Kate White's book *Why Good Girls Don't Get Ahead . . . But Gutsy Girls Do.* A gutsy girl isn't a bad girl. She can be conscientious, hardworking, kind to her subordinates, and respectful of authority. But she also takes risks and doesn't mind charting her own course.

The secret to being fearless, says White, is to practice risk-taking. Start out with something small. Attempt something you've

> ## Knitting with Risk
> "In knitting, as in everything else, you learn as much from your mistakes as you do from your successes." — Pam Allen, Editor, Interweave Press
>
> There is a certain amount of risk when it comes to knitting. How often have you started a sewing project and not finished it? The other day, I cleaned out my yarn room and found ten projects I had started but not finished. I invested the money to buy the yarn and the needles and other supplies, and then, for whatever reason, I lost the enthusiasm for those projects and put them to the side one by one, letting them sit in a drawer. The key to keeping a knitting project going, I have found, is that it can't be monotonous.

never tried before. Volunteer for an extra responsibility at work or ask the local bakery if they'd consider selling your out-of-this-world muffins on consignment. Print off that story you've had buried in your computer and submit it to a magazine. Whatever it is, take a chance. *For God has not given us a spirit of timidity. . . .*

Another tip White recommends that I really like is to "give risk a different name." When we're anxious about something, when we let fear hold us hostage and keep us from moving forward, that's when it's time to look at that fear from another angle. A different perspective. Look closely at whatever you're afraid of. White suggests coming up with a new name for it:

It could be terrifying — or it could be challenging.
It could be foreign — or it could be intriguing.
It could expose your ignorance — or your ability to learn.[2]

My five-year-old grandson, Cameron, was ready for his first day of kindergarten. I phoned my daughter Jenny after she dropped him off to catch the school bus.

"How did it go?" I asked. I knew Cameron was eager to start school, but both Jenny and I had worries about our little Cam riding the big scary yellow bus on his own.

"Another boy spit on him," Jenny told me and then went on to explain that both boys had been in line and some kind of disagreement had broken out. Apparently, the other boy didn't get his way and spit on Cameron.

My heart sank, and I asked Jenny how she handled the situation, since she'd been standing right there.

"I didn't need to do a thing — Cameron took care of it," Jenny said.

In my mind, I had visions of my precious grandson trapped in an impossible situation on his first day of school. "What did Cameron do?" I asked.

Jenny laughed softly. "Cam looked the boy directly in the eyes and said that if he did that, he couldn't be his friend."

Oh, my, I thought. *Such wisdom and strength from a five-year-old boy.*

"By the time the bus arrived, Cameron had a new friend," Jenny said. "They had their arms around each other and were the best of buddies."

Cameron could have easily labeled this little boy a bully and a troublemaker, and refused to have anything to do with him, which would probably have made the situation worse than it was. Or he could have cowered in fear and given in to the little boy's demands, which would have been another negative option. Instead, he courageously chose to give that little boy another name — potential friend — and he treated him accordingly. It wasn't a sure thing that this boy would be his friend; Cameron took a chance — he risked the possibility that not only might the boy not want to be his friend, but he might do something even worse than spitting on him.

In order for our dreams to see the light of success, we must learn to take control of our fears. We need to turn those fears over to God and focus on what's really important: seeing the dreams He's given us come true. See, dreams remain only wisps of enjoyable but useless imagination if we don't give them an anchor to hold to. If we don't make them determined goals. Faith in God is that anchor; it's what enables that dream to come down off the shelf and sit right down in front of us. Since God is the One who gives us our dreams, they are ultimately His for us to hold, but we must be willing to approach them with the mindset that so many successful people have had over the years. We must be ready to attempt something so great for God that unless He intervenes, we are bound to fail.

OVERCOMING DOUBT

Once I got over my fears of being a writer, I still had my doubts — quite often, in fact. It took a long time to break into publishing, and even then, the doubts didn't go away. As I heard one author put it, the good news is you're a published author; the bad news is you're published. You now have to publish again! And again, and again, and again . . . There was risk for me because even though I'd finally seen my dream of publishing become reality, I could still fail at any time.

Doubts will come and go, but just like fear, you can't let doubt stop you from accomplishing your goals. I think many times we all find ourselves in the role of Doubting Thomas. Thomas refused to believe until Jesus showed him His scars from the wounds He received on the cross. John 20:24–29 says:

Now Thomas (called Didymus), one of the Twelve, was not with the disciples when Jesus came. So the other disciples told him, "We have seen the Lord!" But he said to them, "Unless I see the nail marks in his hands and put my finger where the nails were, and put my hand into his side, I will not believe it." A week later his disciples were in the house again, and Thomas was with them. Though the doors were locked, Jesus came and stood among them and said, "Peace be with you!" Then he said to Thomas, "Put your finger here; see my hands. Reach out your hand and put it into my side. Stop doubting and believe." Thomas said to him, "My Lord and my God!" Then Jesus told him, "Because you have seen me, you have believed; blessed are those who have not seen and yet have believed." (NIV)

Remember when I talked about how our purpose and our dreams don't always have to do with the end goal or the result we're looking for? That it's all about the journey? This is part of the journey, friend! Trusting God when we can't see the road map isn't easy, but it's necessary. Just like Thomas, we long to see with our own eyes what God can do. But I'll share a little secret: many times, we could see what God is doing; we're just not looking in the right places.

How many times have you caught yourself on the front porch trying to walk through the door of opportunity, only to find the door locked tight? Do you start questioning God? Do you find yourself asking, "God, what's up? You gave me this dream — why aren't things easier?" So often, though, God is working in unexpected places. Maybe it's behind the scenes, where we can't see. Maybe it's in little ways that we're overlooking. I think we also have to remember whose timing we should be looking at — ours? Or God's?

My cousin Shirley is ten years older than me, and while we were growing up, I didn't know her very well. She lived in Ipswich, South Dakota, on the farm, and I was born and raised in Yakima, Washington.

When Shirley was eighteen, she entered the convent and was a Catholic nun for more than twenty years. In the 1970s, she left the convent. Because she'd taken a vow of poverty, she walked away with very little. No retirement, no savings, no nothing. For years she struggled financially before she finally ended up in Florida. She had left the West Coast, spent everything she had to make the trip across the country, and within three months of arriving had lost her job and found herself living at near-poverty level.

One day she was feeling defeated, lonely, and depressed. Her doubts were enormous! She turned to God and said, "I served You all those years for *this?*" A short time later, Shirley won the Florida State Lottery. Now, I don't necessarily condone playing the lottery when you're having doubts about your dreams, but I also know better than to limit God by saying He can't use the lottery for His own purpose. Shirley now helps support other former nuns; she travels, gives half her money to charity, and is having the time of her life.

Recently, she returned from a trip to a very poor, very closed country where she and a dear friend went through customs with thousands of dollars sewn between two pairs of underwear. While there, they were able to bless and minister to people wherever they went. But this didn't happen in Shirley's timing; it was God's. He answered her dream, but in His way and His timing. Ironically, Shirley used to have a poster in her room that read "When I win the lottery . . . ," and it listed all the things she would do. And now she is doing them. Her license plate, by the way, reads "THK-UGOD."

When we say that we believe God has given us our dreams and then we allow our doubts to surface, our faith looks a bit like when you take a two-liter bottle and fill it half with water and half with vegetable oil. You can shake that bottle forever and mix the two liquids together, but as soon as you set the bottle down, you'll discover that the oil and the water separate. That's because they're not compatible — it's impossible for them to ever mix together. Just as oil and water don't belong together, neither do faith and doubt.

For me, the best way to overcome doubt in my life is to remember God's promises. Here are twelve to get you started:

1. God's presence: "Never will I leave you; never will I forsake you" (Hebrews 13:5 NIV).
2. God's protection: "I am your shield, your very great reward" (Genesis 15:1 NIV).
3. God's power: "I will strengthen you" (Isaiah 41:10 NIV).
4. God's provision: "I will . . . help you" (Isaiah 41:10 NIV).
5. God's leading: "He goes on ahead of them" (John 10:4 NIV).
6. God's purposes: "I have raised you up for this very purpose, that I might show you my power and that my name might be proclaimed in all the earth" (Exodus 9:15–16 NIV).
7. God's rest: "Come to me, all you who are weary and burdened, and I will give you rest" (Matthew 11:28 NIV).
8. God's cleansing: "If we confess our sins, he is faithful and just and will

forgive us our sins and purify us from all unrighteousness" (1 John 1:9 NIV).

9. God's goodness: "No good thing does he withhold from those whose walk is blameless" (Psalm 84:11 NIV).

10. God's faithfulness: "For the sake of his great name the LORD will not reject his people" (1 Samuel 12:22 NIV).

11. God's guidance: "He guides the humble" (Psalm 25:9 NIV).

12. God's wise plan: "We know that in all things God works for the good of those who love him" (Romans 8:28 NIV).

BELIEVING IN YOURSELF

We are created for risk. That means we are created to take chances — to step out of the box society built and explore the vast unknown areas of life that God has made for us.

Most people know that Babe Ruth broke the home run record in 1939, but do you know about the other record he broke? In the same year as his outstanding streak of home runs, he was also the player with the most strikeouts at bat.

Several years ago, I attended a writers' banquet and sat through the awards ceremony. They announced the name of the writer who sold the most magazine articles and, to polite applause, the woman came up and accepted her plaque. The next award was for the person who had received the most rejections that year. To everyone's surprise and amazement, the same woman came up to accept that award as well. As Robert Kennedy once said, "Only those who dare to fail greatly can ever achieve greatly."

When I first decided to be a writer, I sat in front of that rented typewriter each morning and repeated something I read in *The Power of Positive Thinking:*

I believe I am divinely guided.
I believe I will always take the right turn in the road.
I believe God will make a way where there is no way.[3]

See, not only must we believe in God's leading for us, but we must also believe in ourselves. God gives us the root of the dream, but He still leaves us responsible. Achieving our dreams requires several things, and one of the first steps we must learn to master is to believe in ourselves.

When you believe in yourself, something wonderful and magical happens. The confidence that you can achieve your dreams helps generate the physical energy you need to accomplish your goals. I know what you're thinking: *Debbie's listened to Zig Ziglar one too many times. It takes a lot more than that.*

Every journey has to start somewhere, and believing in yourself is the first step toward achieving your purpose. Once you believe you can do it, your mind automatically starts figuring out how it can be done. When you apply Scriptures like "I can do all things through Christ who strengthens me" (Philippians 4:13 NKJV) to your heart and to your life and you say those verses out loud, your own enthusiasm triggers your mind to figure out ways of accomplishing your dreams. If you don't believe me, think of it in reverse. If you tell yourself you can't do something, by heaven, you can't. We're talking about fundamental positive thinking.

If you ever want to test this theory of belief, just visit your closest shopping mall. I have often seen God work in, of all places, the parking lot. I'll never forget the day that my son Dale and I went with my friend Linda Miller and her daughter to the grand opening of Kmart in Port Orchard. It was 1988, and this opening was the biggest thing that had ever happened in our little town. We had a population of five thousand, and, I promise you, there were five thousand cars in the Kmart parking lot that day. There was absolutely no parking anywhere. As we drove around and around, I told the kids that I was certain God was going to give us a parking spot. As I slowly guided the car up and down the rows of cars, looking for the space I knew God was about to provide, the two impatient teenagers in my backseat griped and whined, no doubt certain they were missing some incredible blue light specials.

"I cannot have nonbelievers in this car," I said, and I sharply pulled up to the front of the store to let the kids out. When they jumped out, they had a great view as a lady in the very front spot pulled out and I quickly rolled into the now-vacant space. I looked over at the kids standing on the curb with their eyes wide and their mouths open and had to laugh. It is wonderful the way God works.

My daughter Jenny was with me one Christmas when we decided to go shopping at the mall, and there was no parking to be seen. I said, "Lord, we need a parking place."

Jenny said, "There's one."

"No, God has one that's better," I told her.

In a loud voice, my daughter exclaimed, "And, God, Mom's picky!"

I might have been picky, but we did get a better parking spot.

I've seen this happen again and again in small and large ways. A ticket to a sold-out conference or the perfect dress that came only in either a smaller or a larger size than I needed but fit perfectly anyway. God has answered prayers in much larger instances, too, with people He has brought into my life. When I prayed for a special friend, He moved me next door to another writer, Linda Miller, in the first years I was published, and the two of us became a support and encouragement to each other.

These are both humorous and serious examples of an important principle: If you want your dreams to come true, you must believe that it can happen!

Abraham Lincoln is reported to have said: "People are just as happy as they make up their minds to be."[4] I strongly believe that this concept follows through into other areas of our lives as well. We are as success-ful as we make up our minds to be.

From the first day I rolled a piece of paper into the typewriter, I believed it was only a matter of time before I would be published. I forced myself to believe someone would want to buy my books. I planted the picture of the book cover solidly in my mind — I could see my name on the cover as plain as day.

I also proudly announced to the world that I was a writer. Even though at one time I had refused to tell anyone about my dream, once I made the decision to go after it, you couldn't keep me quiet. I talked to my family and friends and anyone else who'd listen about the terrific plot of my current book. I had the confidence of a multi-published author when I hadn't so much as sold a single word. In retrospect, I'm amazed at my audacity. Each year in our family Christmas letter, I would proudly share how many rejections I'd had that year.

This total faith in myself had a rippling effect on our family, a by-product of my dream that I wasn't aware of until many years later. In the process of believing in myself, I taught my children to believe in themselves, too. They, in turn, believed in me. I was their mother, and I told them someday I was going to publish a book, and they believed me, without so much as a question, because I believed in myself.

While unpacking from a move, I came across a paper that my daughter Jenny wrote when she was eight years old:

> I know a lady who writes stories. She wrote a story about a blind man. Someday this lady is going to sell a book. This lady is my mommy.

Jenny believed in me because I believed in myself. See, in the process of pursuing my dream, I taught my children about goals and the God-given power that the Lord offers each one of us when we use the gifts He's given us. We aren't taking anything away from our families when we pursue our dreams; in fact, I believe we're teaching our children some of the most valuable lessons of their lives.

I was euphoric when it came to writing. I hadn't sold a word of fiction, but I was happy, and because I was so cheerful and content, I was a better wife and a better mother.

Indulge me a moment and allow me to share part of a letter that my son Dale, the runner, wrote to me the year he left for college:

> Mom, I'm so very proud of you . . . proud of who you are and what you do. I wonder if people who run a four-minute mile know how good they are? In a writer's sense, Mom, do you know how good you are?
>
> Millions of people talk about writing and millions try, so in a sense, Mom, you're living those people's dreams.

He went on to say, "I've never read one of your books, but that's beside the point." I found Dale's letter to be incredibly insightful. After I finished wiping the tears from my eyes, I realized that those long years of struggle to become published had been well worth the tremendous effort they cost me.

During interviews, people will often ask me how I was able to hold on year after year and face constant rejection and not become discouraged. I wouldn't be honest if I said the rejections weren't shattering for me. But the answer to that is something I didn't fully understand or appreciate until years later. The Lord sustained me. It was His power, His energy that filled me.

If you're struggling to believe in yourself, please don't forget that God believes in you.

And if He believes in you, you have every reason in the world to believe in you, too.

ON YOUR WAY TO SUCCESS

So far we've talked about the fact that we are created for purpose, we're created for dreams, and we most certainly are created for risk. All these things add up as equal parts in our quest for success. You can't follow your dreams if you don't understand your purpose, and you can't take risks if you aren't passionate about your dreams.

But none of these things can take place if you don't believe in yourself. Many years ago, I read a great book by Rick Pitino called *Success Is a Choice.* I liked it so much that I reviewed it for my professional association, RWA (Romance Writers of America). This basketball coach gets right to the point in the first chapter by saying that before anything can happen, you have to first deserve success.

His theory is that there are no shortcuts to winning . . . or, for that matter, to finding success wherever your dreams take you. Nothing meaningful or lasting can be achieved without hard work. We're going to talk about working for your dream later in the book, and we'll talk more about success in the very next chapter, but I bring this up now because Pitino makes some excellent points about belief and attitude.

Getting published was the hardest thing I'd ever done. Ask any successful entrepreneur, CEO, or celebrity, and they'll tell you that it took hard work and determination to get where they are today. Sure, there are those who get lucky — people whose success falls right into their laps. But I would say there is something important about learning to work for what you dream. It teaches persistence, endurance, and the value of determination in the face of obstacles.

This dream of writing certainly didn't come true easily for me, and because of that I appreciate what I've got. I clung to this dream and worked extremely hard to achieve it. I went the extra mile; I put my heart and my soul into every page I wrote. . . . I still do. I refused to give up. Selling that first book wasn't a fluke or a lucky break, nor was it just my destiny. God gave me the dream, but it was up to me to put my emotions and my action behind it; He wasn't going to do it for me. Very early on I learned to set goals, make sure they were attainable, and not take no for an answer.

This is Pitino's point. *Attitude. Action. Per-*

sistence. That's where it all starts: believing in ourselves and then working hard to make sure our dreams come to pass. It also begins with prayer. I find the more I pray about something, the more my concerns become aligned with God's concerns.

We have to learn to take control of our own lives — to accept responsibility for our success or lack of it. People will sometimes tell me how lucky I am. My reply seldom varies. I'm quick to say that the harder I work, the luckier I get, with God's help. We create our own luck. Together, partnering with God, we have the power and we give it to ourselves.

Please read this carefully: I am not discounting God's power or His control and influence in our lives. But too many Christians settle for the belief that "if it's meant to be, then it will happen." And they sit back and wonder why God doesn't send down, like manna from heaven, the answers to all of their dreams. Sure, God can do that — with God, anything is possible — but I don't believe He uses that method for most of us. He wants us to grow and develop, and He wants to see us mature and learn through the experiences He gives us. And He wants us to be confident and positive individuals. Because if you had to choose between two people to represent you to an audience, who would you prefer? Someone who is a worrier and a whiner and keeps waiting for something good to happen? Or someone who is confident and poised and brings with her an attitude of optimism that touches everything she does? I would choose the latter, and I believe that's who God wants as well. He doesn't want negative, crusty Christians. He wants happy, positive people who love Him and life.

This is where self-esteem and a positive attitude are so important. It makes sense that self-esteem is directly related to how we feel about deserving our success. Like just about everything else in life, self-esteem has to be earned before it can be of significant value. If we strive to develop a strong work ethic and are disciplined, we automatically start feeling better about ourselves. The effort and determination we put into a project and the way we feel about ourselves are all interrelated.

In his book *The Success Journey,* John Maxwell writes that "a dream without a positive attitude produces a daydreamer. A positive attitude without a dream produces a pleasant person who can't progress. A dream together with a positive attitude produces a person with unlimited possibili-

113

ties and potential."[5]

It's Okay to Make Mistakes

My daughter Jody took piano lessons as a child, and I remember a particular piano recital when she was twelve. She was always painfully shy around strangers, so piano recitals were torturous events for her. This particular year, she was supposed to be second on the program, but when it came time to begin the recital, the first student didn't show. Jody was forced to go first.

From my seat in the audience, I watched her go up onstage and sit down at the piano. She was so nervous. She tentatively started her song, and only a few seconds into it, she made a mistake. She stopped. In my head, I was screaming, *Jody! Keep going! Keep going!* But she remained absolutely still.

The whole room was so silent, I could hear my own breathing and probably Jody's as well. Jody's head hung down and she slowly climbed off the piano stool, ran down into her dad's lap, and burst into tears. The whole time, I can remember thinking, *Oh, Jody, if you'd just gone on . . . It's all right; one little mistake doesn't make that big a difference. It's all right!*

I think that's the way God is with us. He wants us to take chances; He wants us to try; He wants us to risk. Because when we do, we take our hands off the steering wheel and we say, "God, You're in control." And it's okay if we make mistakes. It's okay if we fail. But we can't ever stop trying. We can't ever *not* try. Because then we push aside all the wonderful things God has given each of us to help us succeed with our dreams. And then we're taking something away from God.

At the end of Jody's recital that day, I leaned over to our little girl and said, "Jody, would you play your song for just Mom and Dad?" She nodded and wiped her tears away. As we waited for the room to clear, a little old grandma came up with her cane, and in this shrill voice said, "Why'd you quit? You had the best song in the whole recital! Now, get up there and play that song for me!"

So Jody went back up to the stage and played the song perfectly, and by the time she'd finished with the last note, everyone had come back into the hall and gave her a big standing ovation.

As you pursue your dreams, I encourage you to take risks. Be daring. Be adventurous. Be confident in the abilities God's given you. Don't be afraid to make mistakes. Part of understanding our purpose in life is being willing to take the necessary risks that remind us who we're living and dreaming for in the first place. God has wonderful things in store for you if you remember that not only were you created for dreams, but you were created for risk, too.

■ ■ ■ ■

4

CREATED FOR SUCCESS

■ ■ ■ ■

Where can I go from your Spirit?
Where can I flee from your presence?
If I go up to the heavens, you are there;
if I make my bed in the depths, you are
    there.

PSALM 139:7–8 NIV

Never consider the possibility of failure;
as long as you persist, you will be
successful.

BRIAN TRACY

From the day you were created, God's hand
has been on you, guiding you and holding
you fast. If we look at the verses in Psalm
139, we can see several that tell us God
wants us to be successful. He yearns for His
children to succeed in life. But what do we
mean by "success"?

When I talk about success, I'm not necessarily saying it means to be wealthy — you
can buy the most beautiful house in the
world, but that doesn't make it a home. You
can sleep in the most elaborate bed ever
made, but it doesn't mean you're guaranteed a night of peaceful rest. You can have a
lot of people around you, but that doesn't

necessarily mean you have friends. What I'm referring to is something my friend Zig Ziglar calls "success with significance."

You see, over the course of my career and my life, I've recognized it's really true that there are three kinds of people: those who make things happen, those who watch things happen, and those who wonder what the heck happened! Early on I determined that I would be someone who made success happen. It didn't come easy and it didn't come overnight. I had to work hard, be smart, and refuse to give up. I also had to believe that success could be mine.

While working on this book, I've been listening to an audiobook by Steven Scott called *The Richest Man Who Ever Lived.* It's about Solomon and how successful he was. There were many others in the Bible who were successful as well. David was successful; Abraham was successful. They worked from God's principles and God brought them success. I believe that success is a blessing from God — why people frown on it, I don't know. Proverbs 16:3 says, "Commit to the LORD whatever you do, and your plans will succeed" (NIV). God desires for us to succeed; we are the ones who get in the way.

As Christians, many of us have a troubling

relationship with the idea of success. We pray for it, we yearn for it, but then we walk away from it. We change our minds. We say, "Oh, I can't ask for that. . . ." When something successful does occur, we shrug our shoulders and hang our heads in what we think is deep humility, and we say we don't understand why God decided to bless us.

Don't take the glory away from God by summing up success as a freak happening, implying that God didn't know what He was doing. He blessed you because you've used the talents and the skills He's given you! You've worked hard, and you've made the choice to pursue the purpose He desires for you. All of that comes back as credit to God, but so often, we take it away from Him by denying our successes.

One of my biggest sources of amusement is listening to how some people pray. Have you ever heard someone pray this way? "God, thank You so much for the incredible blessings You've given me this past week. Thank You for the raise at work and the new house we're buying and the fact that our daughter just got a full scholarship to the college of her choice. . . ." Chances are, you haven't heard many prayers like that. And you don't hear prayers like that because we typically aren't encouraged to talk about our blessings or our praises or our successes. Instead, the prayers God hears from us most often are moans and groans about our boo-boos, and complaints about everything that's wrong.

I heard a comedy routine years ago about how people use prayer for their own agendas. A man stands up in a church service and, with a booming voice, uses prayer as an advertisement as he says, "Lord, I've got a '57 Chevy for sale; it runs real good, Lord. Help me find a buyer for it, Lord, and let them know I accept cash or check!"

What about the woman who takes prayer time to spread gossip? "Lord, I was sitting in church with my eyes on You, and I saw the way Hazel Mertz looked at Bill Johnston. Lord, You and I both know Bill is a married man. I saw the intentions of her heart, and I know You did, too!"

All joking aside, it's time to get excited about the success God gives us — in our souls, in our hearts, and in our prayers.

EMBRACING SUCCESS

In the Bible, when Paul talks to the people of Philippi, he says, "Do everything without complaining or arguing . . . shine like stars in the universe as you hold out the word of life — in order that I may boast on the day

Knitting on Success

As a knitter, there are some projects that will get you excited from the moment you envision them until the very last stitch. That's how I am when it comes to sweaters I knit for my grandkids. It's similar to when I am writing one of my books — I love the project so much that I wake up every day ready to get to work. Seeing my grandkids wearing the sweaters I knit for them fills me with joy and pride.

I'm known as Grandma Pickle to some of my grandkids. I think it all started from Macomber, which sounds like cucumber, so they call me their Grandma Pickle. I always add little tags to the sweaters I knit that read "Knitted with Love by Grandma Pickle." It's a sign that their grandma loves them, that every stitch I've knitted on that garment is just one more way to show them how much I care. They know who made them that sweater, and they know how much they're loved. And that makes any knitting project I do a success.

of Christ that I did not run or labor for nothing" (Philippians 2:14–16 NIV).

Why run a race if you expect no trophy after crossing the finish line? Why attempt to shine if you quickly cover yourself up with words that dampen what God is doing through you?

If we are truly committed to fulfilling the pattern God has created for our lives, to unlocking the door to our purpose and what He wants to do through us, we must accept the success He is going to bring us. After all, if we deny success, we could be denying God's success through us as well. For it is easier to complain than to create. It is simpler to sulk than to seek a solution. But that's not what God calls us to do.

I love what Paul goes on to say in Philippians 3:12–14:

> But I press on to take hold of that for which Christ Jesus took hold of me. Brothers, I do not consider myself yet to have taken hold of it. But one thing I do: Forgetting what is behind and straining toward what is ahead, I press on toward the goal to win the prize for which God has called me heavenward in Christ Jesus. (NIV)

Our success does not happen when we

seek out awards and recognition. Success happens when we stay faithful to the purpose and the passion God has given us. Sure, success can happen for the disreputable, the greedy, the corporate ladder climbers willing to step on everyone else to get to the top. But is that real success? The type of success I'm talking about encompasses more than just financial victory or power or fame. It involves a balance of achievement both professionally and personally, a wholeness that occurs only when we are pursuing our God-given purpose and not our own selfish ambitions.

We need to be more like Bill Vukovich, the race car driver who won the Indianapolis 500 in 1953 and 1954. This was an achievement that few other drivers had ever accomplished and certainly had not been able to do in Bill's time. When he was asked what the secret to his success was, Bill said: "There's no secret. You just press the accelerator to the floor and steer left."

So put that invisible accelerator to the floor, my friends, and press on toward the prize — for in your case, it's straight ahead. God desires success for us, and He is with us right there in the driver's seat. Get ready for a remarkable ride!

Now that you understand why God has created us for success, and why it's okay to desire success, it's time to talk about how you can achieve success.

When people ask me about how to be successful, I advise them to start appreciating the small successes first. Embrace those small accomplishments, because small ones lead to ever bigger ones.

Early in my career, in the midst of all that rejection I received, I learned the importance of this. My very first sale is a good example of a small success. I sold an anecdote about our son Dale for a grand total of five dollars.

Many years ago, five-year-old Dale was part of the Christmas program at church. His entire role consisted of stepping forward, reciting his Bible verse, and then stepping back. Sure enough, when the time came, Dale flawlessly recited his verse, but hesitated when he forgot the Scripture reference. In a moment of panic, he looked to me, and wanting to help, I cupped my hands around my mouth and whispered, "It's Luke! It's Luke!"

Instantly relieved, Dale's eyes widened and he shouted out, "Luke Skywalker!"

Right there in the worship service we

learned of an entirely new Gospel. Naturally, everyone laughed. This tale has long been repeated in our family with other Dale stories, and it was so cute that I wrote it up and submitted it. A few weeks later, I received a check for five beautiful dollars.

This was the first time anyone had given me monetary compensation for my work. I was ecstatic — success at last! After years of pouring my heart into writing fiction, a church magazine had found something I'd written worthy of publication, worthy of payment. Yes, it was five dollars, but to me it was worth five million dollars because it validated me when I needed it most. It told me someone had found my work worthy enough to actually pay me for it. I sold all kinds of anecdotes and worked my way up to articles on the side while attempting to sell my novels. Those small successes buoyed my spirit. Sure, the money was minimal, but it gave me the emotional boost I needed to keep going.

The Lord wants us to celebrate the small successes along the way. He used these small successes to encourage me and to show me that success comes one step at a time.

Think of success like one of your favorite recipes. One of the things I like to do when

I have time is to cook for my family. One of the family's favorites is Clam Spaghetti, for which I found the recipe years ago in a newspaper article. It's changed dramatically over time as I've found ways to improve it. I know that without the individual ingredients all coming together, the recipe won't work. And the better the ingredients, the better the end result. There is often an order you have to follow as well — mixing the liquids together and keeping them separate from the dry ingredients until it's time to combine. Sometimes it's tempting to leave one or two ingredients out — maybe you forgot to run to the store. But skipping those ingredients, those steps, sometimes makes you miss out on the wonderful, tasty meal the original recipe intended.

It's the same with our lives. Stop and celebrate each of those small successes, each of those little steps we take on our journey to success. Don't skip over them, don't rush through them, but take time to enjoy each as it comes. It will encourage you and, most important, it will motivate you to keep going.

CREATE A MISSION STATEMENT

It is easy to want success — it is much harder to achieve it. I think one of the biggest struggles we have when we try to pursue success is that all too often we go about it in every way possible except taking a direct approach. We veer this way and then we move that way and suddenly, our lives and our focus are all over the map. No wonder we have trouble reaching our goals.

Unfocused lives are complicated lives. We spend all of our time putting out fires we don't want instead of building the ones we do. Have you ever known someone who had a "fire under her"? She was passionate, she was excited, she was moving, she was electric! She probably passed some of that energy off to you as well. But she was also focused. She was deliberate. She had a plan, and she was working that plan.

In order to achieve success, we need to think about what is really important. What's important to you? Is it your family? Is it your job? Is it something you want to do but aren't doing yet? One way to narrow this down is to create a mission statement.

Years ago, I thought about creating such a statement, but I was too busy, too involved in other things, and kept putting it off. Other stuff just got in the way. After all, I knew it wouldn't be easy to put my life in general terms and create a bold declaration by which I was determined to live. I'd toyed with a number of ideas, but they felt clumsy and wordy. Sometimes, the best thing for me is to put the thought aside and let the Lord direct me, so that's what I did.

It shouldn't have been a surprise that I found the answer in my Bible, in Genesis. I was reading the passage in chapter 12 where God makes His covenant with Abram. God tells Abram that He will make him into a great nation and that He will bless him. The last part of one particular verse caught my eye: *"I will make you a blessing to others"* (verse 2, NLT). I read those words twice as they gripped my heart and held me fast. In that instant, I knew. This was my mission statement. It was simple, profound, and direct.

In everything I do, in all my work, in matters personal and professional, I strive to be a blessing to others. We'll talk more toward the end of this book about what it means to be created to be a blessing, but I'll share with you now that everything I do goes through several filters, and one of those filters is my mission statement. If something I'm asked to do doesn't have the potential to be a blessing to someone else, then I walk away.

I understand that not everyone will find their mission statement in a Bible verse. Stephen Covey's organization, FranklinCovey, recommends listing your values on a sheet of paper. What's important to you? Don't give yourself long to answer. Write down the first things that come to mind, because your values will always be close to your heart. Once you have those values, put them into action statements.

If friendship is one of your values, then you might write something like this: "I will make time for the friends I have now, and I will seek out new friends as I meet people along the way."

Your mission statement doesn't have to be set in stone. After all, your *life* isn't! Don't be afraid to come back to your statement and review it — change it when it needs to be changed. But whatever you do, stay the course. Don't give up. This is just one of the characteristics of a successful, purpose-filled woman.

CHARACTERISTICS OF A SUCCESSFUL WOMAN

When I think of successful women in the Bible, I think of ladies like Esther, Deborah, and Ruth. When I think of successful women today, I think of Mother Teresa, Ruth Stafford Peale, and my friend Liz Curtis Higgs. If we look closely enough, we discover that all of these women share several similar characteristics when it comes to being successful.

Successful Women Trust Themselves

Successful women have faith in themselves and their dreams. The successful woman has developed the almost childlike ability to trust that the events in her life work out the way they are meant to — with perfect timing. She believes very deeply in herself. For the woman who has a relationship with God, her confidence comes from the quiet assurance that she is walking according to a divine plan.

She trusts that everything that happens in life serves a useful purpose. This means everything — the good and the bad, the difficulties and the setbacks. Major successes are often preceded by what appear to be difficulties, disappointments, and complications. A successful woman realizes this and accepts that each one of those hard experiences is essential in shaping her into the woman she is today. She trusts that her life will turn out okay.

A story is told about a young man who traveled to a distant city. As he approached the city gates, he came to a wise man standing there. He stopped and asked the man what kind of people lived in this city.

"What were the people like in the city you just left?" the wise man asked.

"Crooks and swindlers looking to cheat me at every turn," the young man said.

The wise man sadly shook his head and said that this city was filled with those same kinds of people. Discouraged, the young man turned away.

Soon afterward, the wise man was approached by a second traveler, who asked about the city. Once again, the wise man asked about the people in the city from where the traveler had come. The traveler smiled broadly. "Generous and kind," he said. The wise man smiled back and told the second traveler that this city was filled with those very kinds of people. The traveler, pleased and excited, hurried to enter the city gates.

As this story demonstrates, life is what we make of it. So many of us are like this traveler. We find exactly what we are looking for in life.

I share this story because I think it is such a strong representation of how we must approach our own success. If we trust ourselves to be successful, then we will look at other people and situations with success in mind as well. If we trust ourselves to be failures, we will see others the same way.

A Successful Woman Accepts Responsibility for Herself

In a famous study by Victor and Mildred Goertzel titled *Cradles of Eminence,* the home backgrounds of three hundred highly successful people were investigated. These people had made it to the top. These were brilliant and ambitious men and women like Franklin D. Roosevelt, Helen Keller, Winston Churchill, Albert Schweitzer, Clara Barton, and Albert Einstein, just to name a few.

The results brought some surprising revelations to the surface. As children, three-fourths of these top leaders were troubled by either poverty, a broken home, or overly possessive, dominating parents. Seventy-four of the eighty-five fiction and drama writers involved in the study and sixteen of the twenty poets came from homes where they saw tense psychological drama played out by their parents. Physical handicaps such as blindness, deafness, or crippled limbs characterized more than one-fourth of the sample group. And yet, from such poor circumstances, God was able to create success.[1]

The men and women listed above all had problems and challenges to overcome as they grew up. I can relate. My childhood wasn't grand or inspiring, either. My parents didn't have time to encourage me, and my teachers didn't see the point in doing so. I was average in the most average of ways, and some might even argue that I was below average. But that didn't stop me from desiring success or achieving it. The day I rented that typewriter and set it on the kitchen table was the day I decided it was time to take responsibility for my success. No one else was going to do it for me. No one else is going to do it for *you*, either.

One of the smartest things a successful woman can do is set goals. And they don't have to be work-related; these goals can and should encompass and span your life. To paraphrase motivational speaker Brian Tracy, any success is linked to a sustained period of *focused* effort toward goals, with the determination and grit to stick with it until those goals have been achieved.

I've been working with goals for more than twenty years now, and I can tell you, the successful woman isn't satisfied with a few indefinite I-hope-I-can-do-this ideas regarding the future. Time, effort, and thought have to be put into each and every aspect of career planning. I have weekly goals with daily priorities, monthly goals, yearly goals, and five-year goals. I keep track of my goals in my performance planner published by Zig Ziglar's company. I've been working with this format for the last fifteen years, and I have found it to be an invaluable tool in keeping me focused. The first part of the planner is dedicated to helping narrow down a long list of dreams and desires into four precise, timely goals. This is what's known as the S.M.A.R.T. plan, and the acronym stands for the following:

Specific
Measurable
Action-oriented
Realistic
Timed

These goals are listed in my planner for me to review on a daily basis, but the planner also assists me in keeping tabs on my weekly goals and daily priorities. Before you can work with this planner or any other, goals must be set. Forget buying the latest electronic gadget and thinking that will get you organized. The key to success is to start with the basics. And that means starting with your goals, and starting with a plan.

Don't make the mistake of thinking you don't need a plan. I'm afraid there's a tendency for people who have the passion and the excitement for something to forget that a plan is also required. That plan is a blueprint for achieving your goals, your hopes, your dreams. . . . And everyone needs one. For every minute you take to plan ahead, you save five minutes down the road. That's a 500 percent return for the time invested.

With my goals already set, I look at my time on a weekly basis and break it down using an ABCDE method for dividing my to-do list into high-priority and low-priority tasks:

A Tasks. An "A" task is something that can't be put off. This is my high priority. For me, it could be writing a chapter or working on a speech for a conference, but whatever it is, it's my top priority for the day. I suggest you create A tasks that are in keeping with your mission statement. Always stay focused on your mission!

B Tasks. A "B" task is one that's important but not as vital as an A task. Maybe I need to read the galley pages for a book that someone wants me to endorse, or some other work-related task. Both A and B tasks have deadlines, but I'm going to get paid once the book is delivered. No one's paying me to give a quote or an endorsement for other books.

C Tasks. A "C" task is something that's nice to do but isn't that important in the overall scheme of things: lunch with a friend, a long phone call to someone you haven't talked to in a while, or running out to your favorite store for a break from what you're doing. It's easy to waste time with C tasks, and I try to do those only once the A's and B's are finished. Everyone needs to relax now and again. Frittering away time won't hurt anyone as long as it doesn't become a habit.

D Tasks. "D" tasks are those you delegate. This applies to work and home. At work, I delegate as much as I can to my assistant so I can focus my energy on what I do best — and that's writing.

Delegation at home is just as important as delegation at work. What are the chores you don't have time to do? Could someone else do them just as well as you can? I have a bookkeeper who manages my family's finances, pays the bills, and handles all the details in our estate planning, incorporation paperwork, and other important record-keeping. Maybe you travel a lot and you're too worn out to clean the house. Find someone to do that for you. Or enlist the help of family members. Whatever you do, remember that you don't have to do it all. All too often we want it all and we want it now, and that makes us think we have to *do* it all.

I learned the secret of delegation from a time-management tape series I listened to by Brian Tracy.[2] The way to figure out if delegating something will work for you is to sit down and calculate what you earn an hour (assuming you work outside the home) and then compare that figure to what it would cost you to pay someone else to do it. Once I did that exercise and saw those figures in black and white, it made perfect sense for me to hire an assistant and to delegate.

E Tasks. "E" stands for *Eliminate*. E's are what I consider huge time-wasters. These are things that creep up in my life, distract me from my goals, and take my focus off what's important. They can be people, places, or things, and I have to constantly be on guard to avoid these.

For a time, I was online every night, but I soon recognized how easy it would be for me to become addicted to the Internet. I now e-mail special friends once a week, and that's the only time I allow myself to be on-line other than for work-related items. Computer games definitely fall under the E category and can be a huge problem for people, especially for writers. Many employers ban games from workplace computers and for a good reason — they get played! I made it a rule long ago that I would never have any such games on my office computer. The temptation to prove my skill and mastery of mahjongg each day could eat up valuable writing time. I actually have a friend who played mahjongg on her computer while she was being interviewed on a live radio program. Now that's a computer game addiction!

The telephone is probably one of the worst time-wasters for me, and that's because I seldom know what to say to get off the phone. I want to be polite, but at the same time, I don't have all day to chat. I've discovered the easiest way to get someone to the point is to ask, in a friendly voice, "Hello, friend, what can I do for you this fine day?" It gets whoever is on the other end of the line to their point quickly.

Another time-waster that many of us experience is procrastination. The best advice I can give you in this area comes from W. Clement Stone. At one time he was one of the richest men in America and perhaps the entire world. He built an insurance empire, and he credits his huge success to three small words: *Do it now.* It's said that he met with his sales staff each morning and had them shout that out in one voice. The next time you're tempted to put something off, think about these words: *Do it now!* Then do it!

Some time-wasters aren't as easy to identify, and the choice is strictly personal. Several years back, my friend Linda Miller and I did a radio show every Friday at noon. It took the entire day, but we loved it. We had a great time and got to be so popular that we were approached about doing a nationally syndicated show. Now, the radio exposure was sure to help our careers, but as we started to focus more and more on the programs, we had to ask ourselves the question: *Are we writers or radio personalities?* Immediately we saw how easy it can be to steer off course. My future wasn't in radio, and neither was Linda's. Make sure you eliminate whatever is in your life that distracts you from your primary goals.

The last thing I want to say about time-wasters is this: Next time something or someone comes along seeking your time, ask yourself, *If I agree and answer yes to this request, what am I saying no to?* If you take on that project at work, what are you giving up? If you agree to organize that event at church, what will you be unable to do at home?

A successful woman knows how to manage her time well, and that means knowing how much she can do and what she should let go of.

A Successful Woman Invests in Herself

I can't emphasize enough how important it is to invest in yourself. Whether you're a stay-at-home mom with a dream of one day doing something big, or a corporate executive striving to make it on the fast track, it's imperative that you give something back to yourself as you travel this journey called life.

I've known women who put in forty hours a week and do what's asked of them — nothing less and nothing more. They don't look ahead to additional training opportunities or motivational conferences. They don't read or study or plan. They rely on others, like their employers, for any chance to improve. While that sounds appealing to some, it's not the road to stellar achievement. If your desire is to find success, the sooner you take control of your life and your career, the more quickly you'll obtain it.

One of the first ways I started investing in myself was by listening to motivational tapes. What I love about listening to books on tape or CD is the freedom it allows me. I can drive and listen to audiobooks; I can listen while I get dressed in the morning and put on my makeup or while I take a bath at night. But I don't listen just for enjoyment's sake. Since I started listening, I have followed the advice that each of those tapes offered. Whether you listen or read, don't be afraid to seek out books that will inspire and encourage you in what you want to do.

A Successful Woman Thinks About Success

It's true. You are what you think. You are what you're passionate about. You are what you . . . are. If you think about success — if you read about it, write about it, live around it, and yes, think about it — you can be successful.

Now, I'm not saying you can think, *I want to be successful,* and poof, you're a success. If you believe that, then you haven't read the first few chapters of this book! What I am saying is that women who think about success are a lot closer to it than those who don't. One of the biggest determining factors is whether you are keeping a PMA, a Positive Mental Attitude. Focus (there's that word again) your attention on the positive. There are those who will find cause to complain in the best of times. Avoid those people. Their negative attitude will drag you down.

I once had an acquaintance ask me to go to lunch with her. It was the worst lunch I have ever had. This woman's daughter had been in a terrible car accident, and she dragged out photos of the mangled vehicles to show me. Then she told me that one of the boys in her husband's Scout troop had been killed in this terrible shooting, a young life snuffed out. As if that weren't bad enough, she told me she'd recently lost her job. As the minutes wore on, I grew more and more depressed. I had to ask, was there *anything* good happening in her life?

"Oh, well, yes, I'm using my severance package to take my family on vacation," she said.

Vacation. That's good. I sighed with relief. Finally, something positive.

"That sounds nice," I said. "Where are you going?"

"Bosnia."

Bosnia! This woman was the Eeyore of the

Hundred-Acre Wood. Yes, life will give us lemons and bad things are going to happen. But the old adage of turning those lemons into lemonade still rings true for me. This woman had an uncanny ability to take lemons and make them into sour grapes.

Stay positive and surround yourself with upbeat, constructive people. Enthusiasm and ambition are contagious. Positive people condition us for success the same way that positive thinking moves us forward to reach our goals.

REMEMBER THE FIVE "BE'S"

Often, the truest signs of success are things that people don't see at face value. The sense of satisfaction and joy I felt the day I sold that first novel has never left me, nor can it ever be duplicated. The morning my agent phoned to tell me I'd made the top fifteen of the *New York Times* best-seller list was another high point because I'd strived toward that goal for so long. Over the years I've discovered, however, that it isn't lists or awards that give me the greatest joy. It's the reader who lets me know that my books have touched her in some way and have made a difference in her life. That's what gives me my greatest sense of satisfaction.

I'll close this chapter by leaving with you

my own personal formula for success, something I like to call the "Five Be's":

1. Be Proud
Take pride in who and what you are because you are special in God's eyes. Deuteronomy 4:32 says, "From the day God created man and woman on this Earth . . . as far back as you can imagine and as far away as you can imagine — has as great a thing as this ever happened?" (*The Message*). You are a unique human being; there's only one in the world like you. Embrace the blessings God has given you, and be ready to give something back.

2. Be Persistent
Go after your goals with everything you've got. Don't give up; it's the people who have the fortitude to keep trying even in the face of adversity who eventually find success.

3. Be Bold
Dare to dream! Each of us can be the person she wants to be. God did not create us with the intention of watching us sit back like sulking alley cats waiting for a handout. He wants us to stand tall, walk firmly, and be excited about reaching the goals He has placed in our hearts.

4. Be Grateful

Appreciate the little things in life. Appreciate the chance to dream and the encouragement you receive along the way. Appreciate the opportunity to learn from your mistakes.

5. Be Yourself

No one ever found success by trying to be someone else. Matthew 23:11–12 in *The Message* says, "Do you want to stand out? Then step down. Be a servant. If you puff yourself up, you'll get the wind knocked out of you. But if you're content to simply be yourself, your life will count for plenty."

Don't be afraid of finding and pursuing success. It is a significant part of the journey in fulfilling the purpose God has for you.

■ ■ ■ ■

5

CREATED FOR
BALANCE

■ ■ ■ ■

If I rise on the wings of the dawn,
if I settle on the far side of the sea,
even there your hand will guide me,
your right hand will hold me fast.

PSALM 139:9–10 NIV

Most people struggle with life balance simply because they haven't paid the price to decide what is really important to them.

STEPHEN COVEY

"You hem me in — behind and before; you have laid your hand upon me" (Psalm 139:5 NIV). I love how this illustrates so perfectly the balance God wants to bring to each of our lives. If you think about it, the whole purpose of why we hem pants or skirts or any other garment, for that matter, is so we can prevent the thread and ultimately the piece of clothing from unraveling. I don't know about you, but many times in life I feel like I'm unraveling! The weight of activities, family, problems at work, or any combination of these can pull at the threads of our hearts and minds. And yet we can be confident that God has hemmed us in; He is protecting us and keeping us, if we only look to Him for the balance we need.

If we are truly intent on following God's purpose for our lives, balance is a key part of the equation, and I believe balance is achievable only when we put God first.

I once heard a story about a woman who took her husband to the doctor's office for a checkup. After the exam, the doctor told the woman that her husband was suffering from a very serious infection.

"What did he say?" asked the husband, who was hard of hearing.

"He says you're sick," said the wife.

The doctor went on. "But there is hope. You just need to reduce his stress. Give him a big healthy breakfast each morning; be pleasant, nice, and kind; make him his favorite meal for lunch and dinner every day, and — this is very important — don't discuss your problems with him; it will only make his stress worse. Don't yell at him or argue with him, and, most important, just cater to your husband's every whim.

"If you do this for the next year, I think your husband will make a complete recovery."

"What did he say?" asked the husband.

The woman turned and looked at him sadly.

"I am so sorry, honey; he said you're going to die."

As women, we certainly have a lot on our plates these days, don't we? So much that life can often seem overwhelming. Not only do we care for our husbands, but we also care for our children, parents, and friends; we manage the household, volunteer in our churches and communities, and many of us work a forty-hours-a-week job as well. It's not just us females — as a nation, we are stressed.

In fact, Gallup did an interesting study a few years ago that showed that 50 percent of adults in our country lack the time they need to do the things they want. It's probably not surprising that more women than men in that group experienced stress on a daily basis, and those who were employed and who had children under eighteen experienced the highest levels.[1]

Go back and look at that statistic again. Half of those adults polled lacked the time to do the things they wanted. But the other half *did* have the time. So how did those folks do it? Everybody has the same twenty-four hours in a day, and yet, there are some who are much better at handling those hours than others. Whether you're talking about success in work or success in life, the key is balance, and, I promise you, we were created for balance.

Psalm 119:1–8 (*The Message*) says that we are *blessed* when we follow God's leading:

> You, GOD, prescribed the right way to live; now you expect us to live it. Oh, that my steps might be steady, keeping to the course you set; then I'd never have any regrets in comparing my life with your counsel. I thank you for speaking straight from your heart; I learn the pattern of your righteous ways. I'm going to do what you tell me to do; don't ever walk off and leave me.

Steady steps. Sometimes it's hard to be steady when we're passionate about something, isn't it? We don't want to walk — we want to run! I have to be careful of that when it comes to my career. I get so excited about writing and talking with my readers and sharing my stories with other writers that I could completely miss out on other things. I could lose out on precious moments in life. But I'm also passionate about those other precious things — my marriage, my children, my grandchildren, even my knitting.

Go back to the verses I just quoted and reread them. Notice the line "I learn the pattern of your righteous ways." I love that. God has given us a pattern to follow when it comes to balance, and we can find it throughout His Word.

BALANCE IN LIFE

So how do we achieve balance? As women, many of us cope and survive by juggling. We fit this in and we make room for that — we keep the weight even by moving this over here and that over there. We multitask better than anyone, but let's face it: God did not form Eve out of Adam's rib for Adam to say, "I will call her *super*woman."

I tend to be a workaholic. That's why, many years ago when I had the chance to rent an office outside the home, I did. It's funny — many writers I know dream about earning enough income from their writing to quit their full-time jobs to write at home. I, on the other hand, couldn't wait for the day I earned enough from my writing to get out of the house!

It was hard in those early days. Writers don't get a paycheck every month, so another writer and I went in on the office

Knitting in Balance

"The simple meditative act of knitting may not bring about world peace, but it certainly has made my world more peaceful." — Ann Budd, book editor, Interweave Press

Evenness, steadiness, and yes, balance, are definitely things we need when it comes to knitting. Neat, even stitches make for a well-crafted garment; stitches that are too tight look bunched up, and stitches that are too loose . . . well, we've all seen afghans with big holes in them where there shouldn't be! Time also has to be balanced when it comes to knitting. Just like anything in life, you can overdo it. You can watch too much TV. You can spend too much time knitting. I can sit for hours and hours and knit on a project. But at some point I have to get up and do something else. Why? On a practical level, eventually I get tired. My arms and shoulders start getting sore, my eyes get tired, and my brain wearies of calculating rows and stitches. When it starts becoming work, it stops being fun.

Most knitting, though, is done in pieces. The project is created in stages, like building a house. I feel a strong sense of accomplishment and balance when I set knitting goals and I don't try to get the whole thing done in record speed. This week I'll finish a sweater for my daughter Jody. I'm almost done with the last sleeve, and then I just have to add the collar. It's a process that takes time and balance to do and to do right.

together, thinking that if one was short on funds, the other would pay the rent until a check came in. I remember signing the lease and knowing this was a trust issue with God. I had to trust Him to provide from month to month. This was a giant leap of faith for me, and yet it was so worth it to me and my family.

I'm a focused person — it's the way I function best — but I learned a long time ago that I had to prioritize and at the same time protect what was most important to me. No one else was going to do that for me.

What are the things that are most important to you and why? Make a list of five to ten things. God, marriage, family, friends, and work are hopefully all in there somewhere.

Once you know what the priorities are in your life, how will you protect them? Will you make a rule that home is home and work is work? Will you banish work from your weekends? Will you insist that Sundays are your day of rest instead of your catch-up day before another hectic week starts? No one will protect your priorities but you. And you must protect them if you want to keep a life of balance.

These days, I have my own office with a staff of three. Work is work and home is home. I've been able to create a space between my home life and my business life. I rarely bring work home with me. My husband, my children, and my grandchildren all know that if I'm home, they have my full attention.

BALANCE AT WORK

Not only is there balance between my professional and personal lives, but I've developed balance in my working life, too. I've learned to create it. At the first of every year, I schedule time for vacations with my husband and time with my children and grandchildren. I map out the months I'm going to be writing and the months I'm going to be on tour or doing other promotional work. This helps me enormously because whatever I'm doing gets 100 percent of me. When I tour for a book, I give it everything, all of me. When I'm writing, my work has my undivided attention. I don't schedule conferences, speaking engagements, or anything else that will draw me away from my book. I try to do the same with family time and with my marriage.

BALANCE IN MARRIAGE

Years ago when our children were still little, Wayne and I went out to dinner. This was rare for us, and after settling into our seats and placing our orders, Wayne said, "You know, all we ever talk about is the kids. Tonight that's taboo. Neither one of us is allowed to utter a word about the children."

We looked at each other lovingly and waited for the other to speak. The overwhelming silence was deafening, and it dawned on us that we had nothing to say! I smiled, reached my hand across the table to shake his, and said, "Hi, my name is Debbie," and we both laughed. Communication in a marriage is so important, but it will never happen if you don't make time for it.

Each winter, Wayne and I drive from our home in Washington State to our winter home on North Hutchinson Island in Florida. In case you're wondering, that's 3,323 miles. Over the years, we've had a number of adventures traveling across country in the middle of winter. We hit a blizzard in Salt Lake City once. Our car has broken down twice and needed repairs. My husband enjoys taking the back roads and stays off the freeway as much as possible, so as a result, we have slept in towns where the largest structure on Main Street was the car wash.

People often ask us why anyone would choose to drive that far. It's a good question, and it took me a long time to uncover the answer. The week it takes to drive between our two homes is one time of the year when Wayne and I are guaranteed quality time together. In this hectic world, it has become more and more difficult to find extended time for each other. If you're married, you can probably relate. Between kids, work, friends, and all the other distractions life brings, like television, cell phones, the Internet — the list could go on — there's not a lot of time at the end of the day for each other.

So, it's in the car on the way to Florida

160

that we can talk without the fear of inter-
ruptions. It's amazing how much we have
to discuss. We may go several hundred miles
with barely a word, or we may chatter
nonstop for miles on end. Each year on the
long drive we fall in love all over again.

I think every marriage needs special time
set aside to communicate. For some, that
might mean a romantic weekend, a stroll on
the beach, or cuddle time on a Saturday
morning, but for Wayne and me, it's 3,323
miles that bring us closer to the Florida
sunshine and each other.

BALANCE WITH FAMILY

We need to have that same kind of focused
intentionality with our children, especially
when they move out of the house. As our
children got married and our family ex-
panded, I discovered that unless we planned
specific times together, the days and weeks
melted away. So, every few months I schedule a special get-together for whoever can
make it. We've rented the local high school
swimming pool, stuffed ourselves at an ice-
cream parlor, gone to a water park, and had
multiple family potlucks. As the grandchildren get older and become involved in
outside activities, this has become difficult
to plan. Still, I make the effort because fam-

ily is important.

Holidays are important, too. I recognize that it's good for our children to develop their own family traditions and special family times, so we try to do "off holidays." We get together the night before Thanksgiving. The last weekend before Christmas, we do a progressive dinner. We also try to do a big family trip around the Fourth of July. One thing I've learned is the necessity to be creative.

For years, my daughters and I had a special getaway weekend, but now that they're young mothers themselves, they have a harder time leaving their families for more than a day, so we adapt. Now we have a slumber party at my house the first Friday of December. We stay up until the wee hours of the morning, baking cookies and making candy for a Christmas Open House that the three of us do together. We have a blast! I schedule time with my grandchildren the same way. Special times with Grandma and Grandpa.

SAYING NO

When you commit to prioritize and protect what's most important to you, inevitably, the N word has to come up: No. *No, I'm sorry, I can't do that. No, I won't be able to help with the bake sale this time. No, I can't talk right now.*

How is it that we let one little word weigh so heavily on our hearts? Kate White, author of *Why Good Girls Don't Get Ahead . . . But Gutsy Girls Do,* quotes Oprah, who says that as women, we have this "disease to please." We want to be liked by everyone. We don't want to let anyone down. We want to keep others happy, and by doing so, stay happy ourselves. But does that really work?

The problem occurs when we put others' needs before our own to the point that we start bumping into our own goals — our own priorities, and the values we hold most dear.

The old saying that you can't please everyone all of the time has truth to it. You can't. And one of the ways we can quickly start cutting back in our "people pleasing" is by learning to say no. "But, Debbie," you say, "I don't want to become completely selfish and self-centered." You're right. I'm not saying we need to say no to everything, but we should say no to those things that aren't benefiting us or don't match up to our values or priorities.

Kate White gives some great tips on how to recognize those things we should decline and how to go about saying no to them:

1. **The stomach test.** If you ever experience any kind of "dull squeezing feeling in your stomach" when asked to take on an added responsibility that will do nothing for your career or for your family, that's a sure warning sign that you should avoid it.

2. **Use an excuse that's "short and sweet."** Tie your reason for saying no to something you're already committed to. For instance, if someone asks you to serve on a committee of some kind, say, "I'm flattered you asked, but I have to say no. I'm already working on this other committee, and I need to devote all of my efforts to making that a success."

3. **Never say maybe.** This is a good one. We don't want to say yes, but we don't want to let the person down who is requesting something of us so we say, "Sure, maybe I can help with that. Let me get back to you." What does that do but drag out the inevitable? The person who's asked you for help sees

"maybe" as an almost positive answer, and will continue to count on you and ask you. If you do eventually say no, that person will likely be upset with you because she'll feel let down after you gave her repeated semi-positive responses.[2]

Think of it this way: Saying no to something that doesn't match up to your priorities is saying yes to something else that does. You're choosing to follow the pattern God's given you instead of adding your own plans into the works. What if I did that with a blanket or a sweater I was knitting? I'm stitching row on row of beautiful stitches, following the pattern, and all of a sudden I decide to add a stitch that's different from the one called for. Maybe it will work — and maybe it won't. It will probably be fine for the row I'm working on, but when I get ready to finish the sleeve or the collar, I'm going to probably end up frustrated trying to figure out the next step on my own.

Look at it another way. A woman wakes up one morning and decides to take the three small tree seedlings she's been growing up a hill to plant. She loads them in a wheelbarrow and sets off for the hill. Her load is light and she keeps a brisk pace.

She's been walking only a few minutes when she passes a neighbor who casually mentions that she has a package that needs to get to another neighbor at the top of the hill. Would she be a dear and deliver it?

Wanting to be helpful and seeing that there's plenty of room in the wheelbarrow, the woman agrees, and placing the slightly cumbersome box beside her seedlings, she walks on, though a little slower, trying to keep the wheelbarrow from wobbling with the extra weight.

Then she passes another neighbor who, upon finding out where she's going, sends along several heavy winter coats she wants to pass on to a friend, also living at the top of the hill. Seeing the woman with the wheelbarrow helping everyone else, yet another neighbor runs out with a box of twelve dozen freshly baked cookies she made for the church, also at the top of the hill. Everything piles into the wheelbarrow.

Continuing up the hill, the woman is hot and tired as she pushes the now-heavy wheelbarrow up the steep road. Her feet start to ache, and she can feel her hands forming blisters under her tight grip of the handles. Her wrists pinch as she tries to keep the weight steady and the wheelbarrow balanced. She's breathing hard and fast now. Her back hurts from bending at such an odd angle, though it's necessary to keep her load moving forward. Halfway up, she sees a small bench on the side of the road, and, carefully parking the wheelbarrow with a thud, she sits for a brief minute of rest.

She thinks about how just a little while before, she was feeling good and ready to enjoy a beautiful morning of planting those seedlings. *Now I'm sweaty, tired, and miserable.* She isn't looking forward to the rest of the trip up. She asks out loud, "But isn't it true that God won't give me anything I can't handle?" *It must just be me. I'm not trying hard enough.*

"You're right. I won't give you anything more than you can handle," she hears God say. "But did I give you the package to deliver? Did I ask you to take those coats? Did I tell you to pick up those cookies? Those were burdens you alone chose to bear."

Matthew 11:28–30 says, "Come to me, all you who are weary and burdened, and I will give you rest. Take my yoke upon you and learn from me. . . . For my yoke is easy and my burden is light" (NIV).

The yoke God gives us is not heavy; it is custom-made for each of us — designed to never wear us out! The burden that we carry when it comes to our purpose and the pattern God has for our lives is never too big — it's just the right size. It's the other things we decide to do on our own that become bulky; they slow us down and leave heavy weights for us to half carry and sometimes half drag. Pastor and author Rick Warren said when we try to do something that's not part of our purpose, we are more easily stressed, fatigued, and conflicted. He writes, "It is usually meaningless work, not overwork that wears us down, saps our strength, and robs our joy."[3]

When we have balance, our steps are light. This doesn't mean we don't have problems. But it does mean we are equipped to handle the problems that come and not get bogged down by other things that will make those problems worse.

TAKING TIME FOR YOURSELF

When we think about finding balance, we often put our attention on everything and everyone else and forget about ourselves. But in order to take care of others, we have to take care of ourselves, too. We can give only so much before we run dry. The person responsible for taking care of me is me. No one else is going to do it. For myself, I know that when it comes time to eat, I'm the first one in line. I don't think many of us would purposely skip eating for a day or two because we haven't got the time, yet when it comes to feeding ourselves emotionally or spiritually, we often fall short.

The four legs that keep a table standing are similar in purpose to the physical, emotional, mental, and spiritual well-being we each need to keep going. Sure, a table will stand if one or two of the legs are missing, but try putting any weight on it, and you'll quickly discover just how weak it is. That's the way it is with us. We can't feel passion for what we want to do in life, whether that's being a great writer, a first-class corporate professional, or an awesome mother, if we're worn out and stretched thin. This means we need to make sure we're getting enough sleep, exercising, taking a day off in the middle of the week every now and again, and spending time with those we treasure most.

We have to take care of ourselves. Whether it's spending time in God's Word or spending time behind a closed bathroom door (sometimes it's necessary to do both at once!), allowing ourselves time to recharge is important. It's not easy — God made us women to be caregivers and nurturers, and it sometimes goes against our nature to care for ourselves, but it's just as important.

Make a commitment right now that you will make time for you. Schedule a weekly standing appointment with your bathtub and soak yourself in bubbles and surround yourself with candlelight. Do as I do, and keep a dresser drawer filled with items that you treasure and can use to comfort yourself when you're feeling blue. In my drawer, there's a letter from my father, an essay my daughter wrote about me when she was eight, and, for pure comedy, my high school diary. Choose things that will bring you joy, and pull them out when you need a joy boost. We need time each day to feed and groom our souls. After all, it is from the soul that we are nurtured and fed. The heart and the soul are the source of all creativity. Take time for yourself. You need it.

GETTING OVER THE GUILT

One of the things that can upset our balance the most is the guilt that so many of us pile upon our own shoulders. We focus our attention on something we want and instantly feel guilty because we think we should be doing something else. We start bargaining and compromising with ourselves until we feel we're really not doing our best with anything.

I constantly struggle with guilt, especially when it comes to my family and my grandchildren. I look at my grandkids' other set of grandparents, who are both retired. The LaCombes recently took the grandkids to the ocean for a whole week. I instantly felt guilty because I knew that would be impossible for me with my schedule. So I have to make sure the time I spend with them is quality time, doing wonderful things together like picking strawberries and blueberries in the garden we planted at our house, or other special things. This helps because I know we're still creating wonderful memories together.

Some of those special memories include the grandkids' birthdays. Instead of giving them one more gift among the many they will be receiving, I like to get a catalog from World Vision and have them go through it and choose a gift to give another child. They're so thoughtful — everyone takes their time looking through the book and picking exactly what they want. One year, my grandson James wanted a special pump that pumps water up from the ground and a soccer ball. Maddie, the granddaughter who shares her birthday with me, decided she wanted to get a camel. It was $700 for the whole camel; $350 for "half" a camel. She wanted the whole camel.

"Maddie, that's a little more than I was prepared to spend, but if you're willing to give me part of your allowance for two months, I'll get the whole camel," I told her.

Maddie scrunched up her nose as she looked closely at the picture in the catalog, and I could tell she was thinking hard.

"Okay, half a camel will do."

That's one of my favorite grandkid stories, and there's a good lesson in it. I could easily have let guilt prod me into giving in to whatever my little granddaughter wanted, but what am I teaching her if I do that? Now, believe me, I love spoiling my grandkids as much as any grandmother does, but I also hope I am instilling in them some of the same goals and aspirations that I saw happen with my own kids as the result of watching me reach for my own dreams.

A BALANCED SPIRIT

I wish I could tell you that by utilizing certain surefire methods of goal-setting and day-to-day organizational strategies, your life is sure to be perfect from this point forward. If that was the case, this book could be called "Debbie Does It and You Can Too!" Unfortunately, no one has the one solution that works for everyone else. God made each of us different. It's not enough to have your to-do lists neatly organized and checked off at the end of the day.

There are many women out there, many of your friends and coworkers, who look like they have it all together on the outside, but inside, they are just as desperate as you to find this thing called balance in their lives. In fact, you may be surprised to discover that they think you are the one who has it all together.

We will talk about this later, in the chapter on worship, but it's well worth pointing out now that balance in life starts with a balanced spirit. How we feel and think on the inside affects what we do for others and what we do for ourselves. It's about our attitude, it's about our outlook, and yes, it's about how we see the world. It's how we view God.

Now, you may have just read that paragraph and are thinking, *I can tell you right now, with the things I'm going through, there's no way I have a good outlook. Life is too hard!*

I have been where you are. I have been in the dumps where I questioned what God was doing, and questioned what I was doing, too. I have wondered which side was up and why all the doors seemed frustratingly locked up tight. But I discovered a secret many years ago that I'm going to share with you.

I chose to think differently.

See, I may not be able to always control my circumstances, but I *can* control my thoughts. I *can* control my fears. I *can* control my attitude. All of this helps in having a balanced spirit.

The reason I know I can control my thoughts, fears, and attitude comes straight from God's Word:

Everything is possible for him who believes. (MARK 9:23 NIV)

I tell you the truth, if you have faith as small as a mustard seed, you can say to this mountain, "Move from here to there" and it will move. Nothing will be impossible for you. (MATTHEW 17:20 NIV)

Come to me, all you who are weary and burdened, and I will give you rest. (MATTHEW 11:28 NIV)

All of these verses are promises from God, promises we can depend on with absolute confidence. It takes work to remember these

174

promises, to utilize them, to internalize them. But do it anyway. It's worth it!

When we approach each new day actively seeking out the good in life — the good in our work, in our children, in our spouse — we will find it. Of course, the opposite is true, too — the negative can be found just as easily, if that's what we're looking for.

I've mentioned it before, but one of the most powerful books I've read, besides the Bible, is Norman Vincent Peale's *The Power of Positive Thinking.* This book helped me overcome rejection and doubt in the early days of my career. I wrote to Dr. Peale in 1982, thanking him for writing his book because it was so very helpful to me as I struggled to sell that first manuscript. Amazingly, he wrote me back. And over the years, I was fortunate to get to know his lovely wife, Ruth. In fact, while I was in the middle of writing this book, I had the opportunity to attend Mrs. Ruth Stafford Peale's one-hundredth birthday party. Mrs. Peale's life is a powerful testimony of God's grace. Many people believe she is the power behind her husband.

Toward the end of his book, Dr. Peale offers some excellent steps that I believe we can apply toward keeping a balanced spirit.[4] He lists many, but I'll focus on only a few:

1. **Practice being relaxed. Easy does it. Don't press or tug. Take it in stride.** It may sound funny to us that we have to "practice" being relaxed, but it's very true these days. As with anything else, we have to be intentional about our spirits. We need to take time out each day to refocus on what's important. That means remembering our priorities, taking time for ourselves, and keeping our spirits balanced and in check.

2. **Discipline yourself not to put off until tomorrow what you can do today.** Procrastination certainly doesn't give us peace of mind; it only builds up worry and distress. By staying on top of things, we have peace of mind, including our attitude.

3. **Take on the "unseen partner."** Remember God's promises and let Him bear your loads. He is never far away.

4. **Determine to like your work.** I'd also add, "Determine to like your life." Look for the good that surrounds you. Look for the people

God has surrounded you with. He's done it for a reason. Embrace each day as if it's your last, and take joy and hope from it.

5. **Get a correct mental attitude.** Dr. Peale writes that the "ease or difficulty in your work depends upon how you think about it." In other words, if you think it's hard, you can be sure it will be hard. If you think it's easy, well, you will find it a lot easier.

We were created for balance. Structure is the key to balance. That means juggling work, family, and friends, and leading all of that should be our relationship with God. I structure time with the Lord every morning and spend time in His Word. I have found that when my relationship with God is right, everything else is much more likely to be the same.

Set your priorities and fiercely protect them.

Don't let guilt trip you up from accomplishing your goals.

Be willing to say no. As Dr. Peale once said, "You will soon break the bow if you keep it always stretched."[5]

We talked about hems at the beginning of this chapter and how they prevent frays and unraveling from occurring. And yet hems do sometimes break. They do get loose and come undone. But thankfully, most hems can be repaired. If you have experienced some unraveling recently, it's my hope and prayer for you that you begin to look for the balance that only God can bring. His Son, Jesus, recognized the importance of keeping balance, in His ministry, in His relationships, and in His time with His Father. Let's follow His lead and remember that we were created for balance.

■ ■ ■ ■

6
CREATED FOR
RELATIONSHIPS

■ ■ ■ ■

If I say, "Surely the darkness will hide me
and the light become night around me,"
even the darkness will not be dark to you;
the night will shine like the day,
for darkness is as light to you.

PSALM 139:11–12 NIV

No road is long with good company.
                              TURKISH PROVERB

If balance is what keeps us stable, it is relationship with others that keeps us thriving. We were meant to have relationships. God created us to long for that connection, for interaction, for kinship. That's why He gives us family; that's also why He gives us friends.

From the beginning, we have had a relationship with God. Psalm 139:7–10 talks about how God is right there with us no matter where we go. "If I go up to the heavens," He is there. "If I make my bed in the depths," He is there, too. If you have ever felt far away from God, the question to ask is not, "Where is He?" but, "Who moved?" He is there for you and for me, longing for relationship and loving the relationship He has with each of us. That's one of the reasons I believe He has made relationships so important for us. This is a key part of our purpose, because more times than not, God brings others into our lives in order to help us accomplish what He longs for us to do.

Just look at all the examples of relationship we find in the Bible: Ruth and Naomi, Mary and Martha, Paul and Timothy, Jesus and His disciples, just to name a few. Each person brought different attributes to the relationship — Ruth had youth and passion while Naomi brought maturity and wisdom; Mary was the listener and Martha the doer; and both Paul and Jesus were teachers, while Timothy and the disciples brought a desire to learn.

Maintaining relationships with others is just as important as eating or breathing. If we don't have people in our lives, we shrivel up and die. But be careful not to seek relationships simply for relationship's sake — the right relationships make all the difference, and it takes time and effort to cultivate those. Right relationships bring positive people together, friends who are willing to be truthful even when it's difficult, who share our values and help us be better people. It needs to be reciprocal, too

— we should offer the same to them. Wrong relationships do more harm than good. Needy people take advantage of those who need to be needed; they require so much care that they sap the other person's energy.

Small towns are known for that feeling of close ties, close friendships. A lot of the settings in my books are based on small-town America. I was born and raised in a small town, and I live in Port Orchard, Washington — another small town. It's what I know and love. My husband was born and raised in a small town, too. I believe that deep down, everyone wants to be part of a community, to share a piece of themselves, to be a friend and to make friends, too. If you think about it, you're involved in several communities already — your church, if you attend one regularly, your neighborhood, your workplace, and even your home. All of these places are opportunities for relationships. It's up to you to seek them out.

One relationship that has always been very important to me is the one I have with my readers. On one of the many motivational tapes I've listened to over the years, I once heard the story of Lyndon Johnson, the consummate politician. He claimed that for every baby he kissed, every hand he shook, every young man's shoulder he touched, he gained ten votes. I remember hearing that and wondering how I could take the same approach as a writer — how could I actually reach out and touch my readers? I decided to ask my publisher about putting my mailing address in my books. In the last twenty years, I've received more than fifty thousand pieces of mail, and probably just as many contacts from my Web site.

I started building my reader list back in 1986 when we produced my very first reader newsletter. Back in those days, I did a letter for every book. When my reader list was around three hundred, I decided to give my readers a small gift to thank them for their loyal support. After tossing around several ideas, I came up with a way to share a part of myself and my family by putting together a small cookbook filled with my family's favorite recipes. My readers loved it, and their response was overwhelming. The following year, I published another cookbook, this time with the recipes my readers had shared with me.

These days, I send out monthly e-newsletters and an annual newsletter and bookmark to all of my readers. I've also taken up blogging (which still sounds to me like something one does with wooden shoes). I faithfully jot down comments and

Knitting on Relationships

I've found that there is a real camaraderie among knitters. I was in an airport once, flying to Omaha and waiting to change planes, when I saw another woman sitting at the gate, knitting. I went over to sit by her, and we started showing each other our projects and discovered that the pattern she was knitting was the very pattern I had lost a few weeks before. After talking some more, we realized that she was a part-time employee at the yarn store where I was scheduled to do a book-signing. She actually came by the book-signing later and gave me a copy of the pattern I'd misplaced. That's a good example of the importance of having relationship with others; that instant connection you have with someone who has a passion that matches your own.

Of course, knitting can come with frustrations, just like the relationships we have with family and friends. I have learned from experience that alpaca yarn stretches. This yarn is extremely soft, durable, very warm, and very wonderful, but it stretches. You have to find an alpaca yarn that's blended with wool. I think this is a great example of how relationships, when done correctly, help keep us centered and alive and not stretched out beyond what we can handle.

Wool is another material you have to be careful of when knitting. I learned this the hard way after spending an entire month making an afghan for my husband. I did it all in individual squares, following one of the most challenging patterns I'd ever done, not once but thirty times. After it was finished, the day came when one of our grandkids got sick on it, so I took this beautiful afghan, 100 percent wool, down to the cleaners to dry-clean. They ran it through the wrong machine, and it went from ten feet across to two feet! So often, we allow the same thing to happen to our relationships. We treat someone wrong or someone treats us badly, and instead of a big quilt of love and respect for each other, we're suddenly left with something the size of a hand towel. We have to take care of what's been given to us, and that includes our relationships.

news on my Web site blog every few days, all for the purpose of connecting with my readers and keeping that relationship going.

I share this with you because for whatever reason you've picked up this book — whether you are looking for the next step in your pursuit of success or are just trying to be a better, more successful, wife, mother, or friend — it's important to remember the people you come into contact with. It's important to keep those relationships, and be a friend yourself. And that's the way I see my readers. I may not change their lives with the books I write, but I hope I improve their weekend. They bless me by letting me bless them.

A LIST OF THIRTY

Many years ago I read *The Aladdin Factor* by Jack Canfield and Mark Victor Hansen, two *Chicken Soup* authors. This was before they were as famous as they are now. The one thing I remember most about that book was something Jack Canfield wrote. He made a list of thirty people he wanted to meet in his life. Entertainers, authors, musicians — people whose work he deeply admired, people he wanted to thank.

He tells the story of running into Red Skelton, someone on his list he had always dreamed of meeting. Jack was walking through the Los Angeles airport when he saw Red waiting by a gate. He hesitated before approaching him but decided that God had presented him with the opportunity, and it was up to him to use it. When Jack approached the famous comedian, he introduced himself by saying, "I'm a fan."

Red Skelton replied, "It's a hot day — I could use one."

The two sat and talked briefly. Jack asked for some advice about a television project he was working on, and Red suggested several ideas that later saved Jack a quarter of a million dollars.

I was impressed. I liked the idea of making a list of my own. Thirty people I wanted to meet in my life. I started out with Pat Conroy, who I think is one of the most gifted writers of our time. Next on the list was Zig Ziglar, an incredible motivational speaker whose tapes I'd listened to for years. Zig was such an inspiration to me that I'd even written a letter to him once, thanking him for helping me learn how to understand and set goals better.

After starting my list of thirty, I laid it on the kitchen table. My son Dale, who was home from college at the time, walked in and asked me what it was. When I told him, he scoffed.

"How are you going to meet Billy Joel?" he asked.

"I don't know. I'm leaving that up to God," I said, somewhat defensively. Actually, I was sort of wondering that myself.

The next morning, Dale had completed my list for me and had written in the names of dead people. He added Mark Twain to my list and then put in parentheses, "Go for it, Mom!" When I asked Dale about it, he gave me a scornful look and suggested I'd spent too much time in the sun.

I muttered something under my breath and headed to my office, where I sat, innocently contemplating my list and thinking that Dale was probably right. It was very likely that I would never get the opportunity to meet anyone on that list.

Then the phone rang and my assistant announced that Zig Ziglar was on the line. He'd saved the letter I had written him more than two years before and now wanted to know if I would appear on an infomercial with him and Lou Holtz. I assured him I'd be honored to and then raced home, threw open the front door, and shouted, "Stand back, nonbelievers!"

Since then, I've met eighteen of the people on my list. I was on *Dallas This Morning* with

Michael Crawford, I was on the radio with Mark Victor Hansen, and I met up with Elizabeth Berg at a writers' conference. When Zig was in Seattle for a Peter Lowe seminar, he invited me into the green room with him to chat before he went onstage. While we were chatting, who should walk in but George Bush (the first).

I have to tell you: that one phone call from Zig had a curious effect on Dale, my doubtful son. The next thing I knew, Dale had a list of his own. The name at the very top of Dale's list is Steve Prefontaine, considered to be one of America's greatest distance runners. There's no way Dale will meet him this side of eternity. Steve was killed in a tragic car accident twenty-three days before Dale was born. Dale is a runner, and if not for a horrible skiing accident, he might have been an Olympic contender.

Every paper he ever wrote in school was on Steve Prefontaine; he's interviewed Steve's track coach, his roommates, and his friends. When Dale was a college junior, he decided he'd use the occasion of Steve's birthday to relive his hero's life. Dale and his best friend took a road trip to the University of Oregon and toured the facilities, reliving where Steve won four consecutive NCAA titles in the five thousand meters. They went to the track where Steve ran, visited the display of his trophies, and then drove to Coos Bay, where Steve was born and raised.

They were taking a picture of the house where Steve grew up when an elderly man stopped them and asked what they were doing. Dale went into great detail and explained that this was Steve Prefontaine's childhood home. He recounted all the marvelous accomplishments Steve had made before his death. The man said he knew all that; he was Steve's father.

Mr. Prefontaine invited Dale and Andy into his home, took them up to Steve's bedroom, and let Dale try on his hero's letterman's jacket. Then he took Dale's picture and invited the boys to stay for dinner.

My son came as close as it was possible on this side of heaven to meet Steve Prefontaine.

GOD'S LIST OF THIRTY

After I wrote out my list of thirty names, it wasn't long before I had a second realization. I was telling God that this list of thirty, these people whom I wanted to meet, all had talent, ingenuity, and a work ethic I deeply admired. Yet, as I met these people whose work I so respected, I learned another valuable life lesson. Many proved to be disappointments, high on themselves and self-centered. The difference I discovered was God. I found that unless they had made God an important part of their lives, they were self-absorbed, sometimes selfish, and, frankly, a disappointment.

I complained to God about this after one such meeting. I was disappointed and disillusioned. I'd met someone I'd looked up to and discovered the person was nothing like the man I thought I knew. That was when God stopped me. He told me I'd asked Him to send these thirty people into my life, and He was happy to do that. But He had another list He wanted me to make. Only this time I was to leave those thirty spaces blank. These were people *He* wanted me to meet.

Have you ever had someone come into your life at just the right moment and you instantly click? Lillian Schauer rented an office space close to mine back in the early 1990s, and we became instant friends. Lillian has lived an incredible life. Married at fourteen, a mother at fifteen, she raised her family, completed her education, and then went on to attend law school. She came into my life at a time when I badly needed a friend, and she has been one of my closest friends all these years. We're so alike, it's bizarre. We like the same food, we read the same books, and she is part of my Breakfast Club (more on that later).

When I meet someone these days, I give him or her a second look because I'm never quite sure if this is someone else God is sending into my life. I'm looking for and expecting the very best. This is part of the reason I know the group of friends I swim with so well. When I first started going to the local swimming pool for exercise, I discovered that most of the people there were in their seventies and eighties. No one really talked to anyone else. So one morning, as we were all standing around waiting for the pool to open, I introduced myself — to every single person. From that time forward, I made a habit of greeting everyone by name. Soon everyone was chatting and talking, and we've been a much closer group ever since. I've made some wonderful friends as a result. In fact, we get together every December at my home for a Christmas Tea. It's so much fun seeing what my friends look like wearing clothes.

So I have my list of thirty, but I also have God's list of thirty right next to it — a sheet of paper with blank spaces numbered from one to thirty that gets me excited every time

I glance at it. This list makes me stop and think: *Who does God want me to meet today?*
Who does God want *you* to meet today?

SEEK OUT ENCOURAGERS

When you expect the very best in people, you'll find the very best. It is so important to surround ourselves with positive people. If we're friends with people who dream big and who believe in themselves, it'll raise the level of our own thinking. It's also important that the people we're friends with be blessings, not barricades. There are far too many naysayers in this world. You and I need friends who will encourage and motivate us to keep going!

Encouragers can be anyone, like your husband or your mother, a sister or a dear friend. I have a number of encouragers. My fiction editor, Paula Eykelhof, has been working with me for almost twenty-two years. I like to tell people that Paula and I are like Annie Sullivan and Helen Keller — only we're not sure which one is which. We're a good team, and we balance each other out. She knows my strengths and my weaknesses, and she's able to draw out the very best in me as a writer and storyteller. Paula's dedication, support, insight, and wisdom have guided me through my books and through the years. We share an incredible publishing history and have forged a strong friendship. Paula works just as hard as I do and is a masterful editor. I believe our partnership shines in my books.

My husband and I have been friends with the Frelingers for more than thirty years. Sharon was the first one to encourage me to go after my dream of writing novels. Back when our children were young, we walked through the park for exercise. I would tell Sharon the story ideas I'd gotten from reading Harlequin Romances.

"Why don't you write those stories yourself?" she asked me one day.

I gave her a long list of reasons why I couldn't, wouldn't, and shouldn't.

She looked at me. "You must not want to be a writer very much," she said and left it at that.

Oh, but I did want to write. I desperately wanted to create my own stories, but I needed someone like Sharon to encourage me to go after that dream.

In the years since I've started writing, Sharon has never stopped being an encourager. At every crossroads she's been there to cheer me on.

My friend Barb Dooley is my spiritual mentor. She prays for me and encourages me in the Word. When there's something heavy on my heart, I contact Barb, and she sends me to God's Word and shares her own life experiences with me. I feel incredibly blessed to have her in my life.

Who's the encourager in your life? Recognize who it is and then nurture that relationship. Let that person know how much you appreciate her loyal support and then find ways in which to encourage her.

Another great thing about encouragers is that, typically, these are people who love to share your good news. You know what I'm talking about. There are people you can pick up the phone and call when something great happens, and there are people you tend to avoid.

I've learned valuable lessons about friends over the length of my career. Some of those lessons have been painful ones. I believe it was Lily Tomlin who said, "When good things happen, the hardest part is finding someone who's happy for you."

There's plenty of jealousy out there, and it's a valid human emotion. When something wonderful happens to someone else, there's that initial reaction — we're ready to stand up and cheer, and then almost right away that feeling comes over us: the nagging question of *Why can't that happen for me?*

One of the most valuable lessons I've learned in the last few years is not to call my friends, at least my writer friends anyway, and tell them good news about my publishing career. The last time I picked up the phone and called a writer friend for this reason was probably sometime in the early nineties. I was excited, but after I got through spilling my good news, there was silence on the other end of the line.

"When's it going to be my turn?" she asked quietly. She was being honest, but it still hurt. And I didn't have an answer for her. I knew then, however, that I had to be more careful about whom I shared my success with.

I was in New York a few years ago at a writers' conference when I got the news that one of my books had been optioned for a movie. I told my editor and my publicist, and if I told anyone else I don't remember, but I rather doubt it. This isn't the kind of news I typically like to broadcast. In fact, I've learned that it's always better to let others do it for me.

I have one writing friend whom I do discuss these matters with. She's a multiple *New York Times* bestseller with numbers that far surpass mine. I chat with her once or twice a year. I consider her my mentor, and she was the one who suggested that if something really wonderful happens in my career, I should share the news only with writers who've had similar success. I have taken that advice to heart and followed it faithfully. It's the same with selling a house or getting a promotion at work. You have to consider the circumstances of the people you're sharing the news with — if good things aren't happening for them, I wouldn't share it unless you know beyond a shadow of a doubt that they are indeed encouragers.

While you're looking for encouragers, be sure to avoid toxic relationships. There are people all around you who will bring you down if you let them. These are people who depress you whenever you're around them, people who make you feel guilty. For whatever reason, these people bring the bad stuff out in you. I have someone like that in my own family, and I've backed away from her as a result. I feel bad, and I don't like it, but toxic people bring their negativity to everyone and everything, and they will bring you down as well.

Seek out encouragers and seek to be an encourager yourself.

If you are married, you know that marriage is the closest, most intimate relationship you will have in your lifetime next to your relationship with God. And yet, this relationship is probably the hardest to keep. The statistic is sad and tiresome to hear, but unfortunately it hasn't changed much: more than half of all marriages in the United States end in divorce. The likelihood of married adults getting divorced is identical among born-again Christians when compared with those who are not born again.[1]

Perhaps more couples could be like the couple who recently celebrated their fiftieth wedding anniversary. They summed up the reason for their long and happy marriage this way: The husband said, "I have tried never to be selfish. After all, there is no 'I' in the word 'marriage.' " The wife said, "For my part, I have never corrected my husband's spelling."[2]

There are no two ways about it: my husband, Wayne, and I are proof that opposites attract, because we certainly are as different as any two people can be. He's introspective and quiet; I thrive on being around people. Wayne comes from a small family; I come from a large, extended family with lots of cousins. Wayne's a night owl and I'm a morning person.

For His own divine purposes, God brought the two of us together, and for the most part, we've managed to accept each other's strengths and weaknesses over the course of our marriage, though we haven't been without our share of problems.

I remember one weekend when I wanted to go to a movie and Wayne didn't, so we stayed home. I wanted to invite friends over for dinner. We ended up watching television — just the two of us. Then a big 9/11 display came to Tacoma that I wanted to go see. Wayne didn't. Frustrated, I went without him, grumbling the entire way. I wasn't quite done being upset when I was dressing for church the following morning. Wayne came with me, and after the singing — I sang, Wayne didn't — our pastor, Kevin Hestead, began the sermon.

I don't remember the topic now. In fact, I don't think I can even tell you which Bible passage he preached on. All I *do* remember is one particular zinger: *The grass isn't greener on the other side of the fence; it's greener where it's watered.*

Wayne looked at me, and I looked at him. He smiled and so did I. I offered him my hand, and we both scooted closer together. You see, we know what it means for a relationship to require watering. Not many people know that in 1989, shortly after our twentieth anniversary, Wayne and I separated for eighteen months.

Like most marriages that come close to or end in divorce, there were festering issues that needed to be dealt with. God worked on both of us during that time. Wayne had moved to another state, and for that entire year I spent one hour a day on my knees. That was my goal, one hour a day. I prayed for Wayne, for my marriage, and for our children. Surprisingly, though I had always considered myself an optimistic person, I didn't feel that way about my marriage. I was certain that our relationship was over.

A week before the divorce was to be final, Wayne called me. He told me he didn't want to go through with it. By then I was emotionally prepared. As far as I was concerned, it was too little and too late. I hadn't seen or heard from him in months. Frankly, I was ready. But Wayne wouldn't give up.

"All I ask is that we put the divorce on hold," he said. "I'm going to move back and we'll give it another shot."

I agreed, though I was wary of getting my heart broken again.

Wayne moved back and we started dating again. We worked out the issues that had separated us in the first place, and that autumn of 1990, he moved back in. Our marriage, with God's help, was slowly healed.

My husband did something very wise before he moved back into the house. He sat me down to talk.

"We have opened that door, Debbie, the Big D door, the divorce door," he told me. "We can start going back and forth and let it be a swinging door, or we can lock it shut forever. Let's never mention that word again. Divorce is not an option. If we get back together, it has to be forever."

We made that commitment and this year celebrated thirty-eight years of marriage. While we've had our ups and downs, as every married couple does, I am thankful for my husband — his quiet strength and his love. I've learned that love is a decision, renewable every day. Every minute, sometimes!

There are some situations where someone really does need to leave a marriage. But then there are others where you can learn and grow and get through it. It's rough while you're in the midst of the hard times, but it's so worth it on the other side. Too many times, we give up when we should keep going. We start thinking about *our* needs and *our* feelings instead of looking at the bigger picture. When the wedding vows are made, it's not just between two. It's between three. Husband, wife, and God, the Creator of them both.

As the pastor said, it is so important that we water and nurture our marriages. Marriage requires loving when we don't feel like loving, talking when we don't have anything to say, and listening when all we want to do is get our own word in.

Dr. Emerson Eggerichs is the author of *Love & Respect.* This is a fabulous book I highly recommend reading. He gives some great insights into this relationship we call marriage. His theory is that most marriages find themselves on the "Crazy Cycle" — and he defines craziness as "doing the same things over and over with the same ill effect." He offers a great example of someone coming into a room, flipping a light switch, and after discovering that the light doesn't work, standing there and continuing to flip the switch back and forth despite never achieving the desired result. What would you think about this person? He's a little crazy, perhaps? That's what I would think.[3]

Dr. Eggerichs compares that scenario to how we treat marriage. I do my thing, my husband does his thing, I aggravate him, he aggravates me, no one ever changes, and the marriage springs a leak and begins to sink. He cites Ephesians 5:33 — "However, each one of you also must love his wife as he loves himself, and the wife must respect her husband" (NIV) — and points out that most of us focus on the love but forget about the respect. I want my husband to love me, and when he doesn't, I don't show respect. My husband wants respect, and when I don't show it, he doesn't show love. Like Eggerichs says, it's a crazy cycle.

In order to get off the crazy cycle, couples have to understand what men and women each want (and, by the way, we do often want different things, or the same things but in a different order). It's that whole "Mars versus Venus" line of thought, and yes, I think sometimes we are that different. We can come together, but it can't be 50/50. Husbands and wives need to commit to each other 100/100.

Above all other relationships in your life, make sure you give priority to your marriage. God can do incredible things in your and your husband's lives if you let Him work. I can testify to that.

As women, we tend to care for everyone else's needs before we see to our own. As a result, we often become depleted emotionally and spiritually without recognizing what's happened or why. When I was a young mom, I just assumed that everything would get easier once the kids were out of the house. I'd have all this extra energy, and huge blocks of time would immediately become available to me. I'd be able to take on some of the projects I'd been putting off for years. Let me tell you — that is definitely a myth! If anything, I found myself more involved in my career and taking less and less time for myself.

My youngest son is now over thirty, and I still haven't stopped to smell the roses, though I am working on getting better at it. Many years ago I learned that I am not the only one in this situation. There are other women out there starving for emotional and spiritual nourishment as well.

Ten years ago, I contacted a friend I hadn't seen for several months. She'd lost her only son in Desert Storm, and while her political career had blossomed, I knew she had struggled in her marriage. Talking with her, I learned that Carol hadn't been in touch because she was in the middle of a divorce. It dawned on me that she had cut herself off from her friends and isolated herself at a time when she needed those friends most. That same week, I had lunch with Lillian Schauer, the attorney friend I mentioned earlier in this chapter. She was one of the most respected attorneys in the county. As we chatted over lunch, she shared a deep pain in her life, one she struggled with, and while she worked in an office dominated by other women, everyone expected her to be strong — she wasn't allowed to be vulnerable or show any signs of weakness. By the time lunch was over we were both in tears.

After these two separate but very similar encounters with friends, I thought about other women friends I knew in the community. Six powerful women, all successful in our careers, all overachievers with type A personalities. Each of us was a success professionally, and yet we were so emotionally depleted that we no longer knew how to take care of ourselves.

I held a tea at my house and invited each of these powerhouse friends over and suggested we support one another. There was Lillian, the attorney; Betty, a bank vice president; Diana, a social worker; Stephanie, a business owner; and Janelle, a real estate broker. We had such a good time together that we set Thursday mornings for breakfast at a local restaurant. We became a prayer group, a support group, and advocates for one another. We chose 2 Timothy 1:7 as our guide: "For God has not given us a spirit of fear and timidity, but of power, love, and self-discipline" (NLT).

We became the Breakfast Club and have been meeting for more than a decade now. I've learned so much from these ladies and am proud to call them my friends. They are certainly my heroes. My friends held my hand when I struggled through contract negotiations when changing publishers. Over the years, they have listened and advised, counseled and encouraged me. When my book *Promise, Texas* hit the *New York Times* best-seller list, it was my Breakfast Club members I contacted first.

A club like that is a great sounding board for all of the hurts and worries and problems you can't necessarily bring to work with you or talk about in the office. We all have these quiet hurts, and the group allows you to share them in an environment that is safe. We wept together when Stephanie developed ovarian cancer and died within five short months, and celebrated when Betty, a widow, met a wonderful man and remarried. When one of my sons was having problems in his marriage, this is the group I talked to. When the son of one of our friends in the group left his wife and children for another woman, it devastated her and she brought it to the group for support. As she and her husband worked through it, we saw every stage through the Breakfast Club. We laugh together, cry together, and often we do both at the same time. I don't share my successes with other writers, but I share them with my Breakfast Club. They're the only group I do.

When you find a group of ladies to build those close, intimate relationships with, you develop extremely strong bonds. It becomes a deep sisterhood. Over the years we've lost some of the original members to job transfers and even death, but the Breakfast Club is where some of my most treasured relationships come from.

If you are struggling with finding good solid relationships with other women, let me encourage you not to give up. The hectic pace of today's lifestyle can sometimes limit our opportunities. We can meet other women in similar stages, but like anything else in life, we have to be intentional. And don't try to convince yourself that you don't need other ladies in your life. You do — we all do. As we seek to fulfill the purpose God has put on our hearts, we need to learn from the experiences of others who have been there. We can share our own experiences with those who have not. We need to come together to pray for one another, through good times and bad. I think Satan finds overwhelming satisfaction when he keeps us from one another, for he knows how much better it is when sisters in Christ are together. Don't let him have that satisfaction.

For where two or three come together in my name, there am I with them. (MATTHEW 18:20 NIV)

■ ■ ■ ■

7

CREATED FOR THE WORD

■ ■ ■ ■

For you created my inmost being;
you knit me together in my mother's womb.
PSALM 139:13 NIV

Nobody ever outgrows Scripture; the
book widens and deepens with our years.
CHARLES H. SPURGEON

In Psalm 139:17, the psalmist talks about how precious God's thoughts are. I believe there is no better place to go to discover God's thoughts and His directions for our lives than to His Word. We were created for the Word.

For me, going to the Word each day is like taking hold of an anchor. It grounds me and roots me so deeply in God's love and grace. When you read and spend time soaking in God's messages, your spirit and your personality are affected in such a positive way. . . . Like we just talked about, the relationship we have with God will grow and flourish.

I have several friends who live quite far

from where I do, and we have to make a determined effort to maintain our friendship. It's the same with God. The words we read in the Bible, His Word, are God's letters to us, and they can change our lives and guide us toward our purpose.

As a writer, words are both my passion and my pursuit. I use words every day to communicate the thoughts, feelings, and actions of the characters in my stories. Words can be effective or ineffective. Robert Frost said that "half the world is composed of people who have something to say and can't, and the other half who have nothing to say and keep on saying it."[1]

Words are helpful, and words can be a nuisance. They build up, and they tear down. Words inspire and encourage — they can also defeat and deflate. Words may sting, but they also soothe. Words take us on a journey of discovery and imagination; they teach us what we don't know, take us to places we never knew existed, and compel us to keep learning.

Some words are powerful; they provide focus and resolution. Every year, each of the ladies in our Breakfast Club chooses a personal word for the year. Maybe you do this or you know of others who do. Last year, my word was *wisdom.* The year before that was *believe,* and the year before that was *purpose* because I had recently read *The Purpose-Driven Life.*

This year, the Lord gave me the word *hope.* Right about the time I was thinking of what my word for the year should be, the pastor's sermon one Sunday was on hope. I went shopping at Wal-Mart, and there was a devotional book about hope. I ran into a friend who introduced me to her friend . . . Hope. I thought, *Okay, God, I get it — hope!* I love watching for the ways God uses that word in my life throughout the year and how He helps me grow as a result.

Despite all my struggles with dyslexia, I enjoy reading. I read and listen to many different kinds of books, both in print and audio format — business books, motivational books, the latest best sellers.

However, there is one Book in particular that I read every day without fail. It has approximately 1,189 chapters; 783,137 words; and it was written by more than 40 different authors. In its pages, it offers 1,260 promises, and it has been translated into almost as many languages.

This Book attracts readers for its stories of drama and suspense, passion and romance, deceit and betrayal, heroism and heart. It's also where you'll find the Greatest Story Ever Told.

HEARING GOD'S VOICE THROUGH HIS WORD

Shortly after I became a Christian, my neighbor Marilyn Kimmel used part of her tithe to send me to Basic Youth Conflicts, now called the Institute in Basic Life Principles. It was a course designed to teach practical life application from a biblical perspective, and before we left, the instructor, Bill Gothard, asked us to make a vow that we would read our Bibles every day. As a brand-new Christian, I was hungry — really hungry — for God's Word. I wanted the meaning from it; I wanted the meat. I made a promise to God that I would read my Bible every day, and I have kept that promise for more than thirty-five years. I know it may sound strange to some. I know that many people struggle with reading their Bible every day, starting and stopping as life gets in the way, but it's never been like that for me. I'll tell you why.

When I read the Bible, that's when God speaks to me. Through His words, I hear His voice, loud and clear, in my heart and my mind and my soul. His Word is the rudder of my life; it's the light of my life. It's also what keeps me grounded and filled with purpose. God's Word is the one thing

216

that's key to what I do and who I am.

When I think about Scripture that speaks to me, I think about Paul's incredible prayer for the Ephesians (3:14–21). The words fill my heart every time I read them, and often I am so stirred that I have to say them out loud.

> For this reason I kneel before the Father, from whom his whole family in heaven and on earth derives its name. I pray that out of his glorious riches he may strengthen you with power through his Spirit in your inner being, so that Christ may dwell in your hearts through faith. And I pray that you, being rooted and established in love, may have power, together with all the saints, to grasp how wide and long and high and deep is the love of Christ, and to know this love that surpasses knowledge — that you may be filled to the measure of all the fullness of God.
>
> Now to him who is able to do immeasurably more than all we ask or imagine, according to his power that is at work within us, to him be glory in the church and in Christ Jesus throughout all generations, for ever and ever! Amen. (NIV)

Isn't that beautiful? Aren't those verses a

wonderful reminder of God's love?

Proverbs 4:11 is another favorite verse of mine, probably since I've had to make several weighty decisions lately: "I guide you in the way of wisdom and lead you along straight paths" (NIV).

To me, it's not extraordinary that I read His Word every day — it's as natural to me as brushing my teeth. It's a part of me. It's what I do.

BELIEVING WHAT WE READ

That's why I can confidently say that we were created for the Word. And not just to hear it or to read it as we would read one of our novels at the beach or, perhaps in the case of some, like a college textbook. We were created to soak in it, inhale it, live it, *be* it. Hebrews 4:12 says that the Word of God is "living and active" (NIV).

Many have described the Bible as "basic instructions before leaving earth." God's Word is our blueprint for living! If you're looking for God's pattern for your life, you need go no farther than your Bible. It's all there if you'll only take the time to look.

Of course, to *be* it, reflecting it and living it, requires *believing* it is the inspired Word of God. I know there are many people, even

Christians, who have trouble accepting that the Bible is completely accurate. They say, "Well, men are the ones who wrote it, so it's fallible," or they look at certain parts and say, "That was for the culture back then." They want to take the parts they like and leave the parts they don't. But I don't believe we can do that.

I like how pastor and speaker Voddie Baucham uses logic to explain how the Bible is truly God's infallible Word. He says that when we're talking about the origin of the Bible, we basically have three options:

1. Men were the source of the Bible.
2. Satan was the source of the Bible.
3. God is the source of the Bible.

Baucham explains that if men were the source, then they were evil men attempting to deceive people, the same men who wrote documents that gave them no power and ultimately got them killed; or, if they were good men, they lied, which eliminates the possibility that they were ever really good.

If the devil was the source of the Bible, than Baucham says that Satan invented the only thing that challenges human allegiance to him — God. That would mean the devil also painted himself as the villain and revealed to us the only means by which we can resist and defeat him. Why would he do that?

It comes down to this: God is the source of the Bible. That's the only conclusion we can draw.[2]

So once you've realized that the Bible is true, that it really does hold the answers to life's questions, why wouldn't you want to read it? Maybe it's a question not of whether we believe it but of how we see it. Do you see God's Word as the source of truth or as a Magic Eight Ball in book form?

OUR SOURCE FOR TRUTH

Too many of us use the Bible to bail us out with the Finger Test. You know the one. You're at the end of your rope so you sit down with your Bible, close your eyes tight, pray a quick prayer, flop open the Book, and point to a verse that you just know is destined to solve your problem.

That's what happened in a story I heard of two old friends who met one day after many years apart. One had attended college and was now very successful, while the other friend had never had much ambition and never made it to college.

The successful one asked his old friend, "How has everything been going with you?"

"Great," said his friend. "One day I opened the Bible at random and dropped my finger on a word and it was *oil*. So I invested in oil, and boy, did the oil wells gush.

"Then another day I dropped my finger on another word and it was *gold*. So I invested in gold and those mines really produced. Now, I'm as rich as Rockefeller."

The successful friend was so impressed that he rushed to his hotel, grabbed a Gideon Bible, flipped it open, and dropped his finger on a page.

He opened his eyes and his finger rested on the words "Chapter Eleven."

The Finger Test doesn't always work, does it?

I'll tell you what does work: consistent time with God. Because the more we do it, the easier it is. But it has to become part of you, and that requires time — intentional moments when you choose to be with God.

George Mueller once wrote:

It is a common temptation of Satan to make us give up the reading of the Word and prayer when our enjoyment is gone; as if it were of no use to read the Scriptures when we do not enjoy them, and as if it were no use to pray when we have no

221

spirit of prayer. The truth is that in order to enjoy the Word, we ought to continue to read it, and the way to obtain a spirit of prayer is to continue praying. *The less we read the Word of God, the less we desire to read it, and the less we pray, the less we desire to pray* (emphasis mine).[3]

When I first started reading my Bible, I would read little bits and pieces and memorize Scripture. More than ten years ago, I memorized the entire book of Philippians and then the first four chapters of Ephesians, but I discovered that I didn't retain it very well.

My goal each year is to read the Bible all the way through. I've done it for the last six years since discovering Bruce Wilkinson's *The Daily Walk Bible.* I didn't care for the traditional annual Bible reading method of taking a passage in Old Testament, the New Testament, Psalms, and Proverbs. *The Daily Walk Bible* starts at Genesis, goes through Revelation, and once a week reviews what you've read. It also comes with a devotional that explains what you're reading. Each year, I read a different version of the Bible, which helps keep its words fresh and meaningful. I love *The Message* and the New Century Version. This year I'm reading *The*

Message and the New International Version side by side. Whenever I come to a passage I don't understand or I'd like more insight into, I immediately see how *The Message* says it as compared to the NIV.

Four Words We Find in the Bible

As a writer, there are four words I use as criteria for every story I write. I have them under the glass top that covers my office desk. Whenever I begin thinking of a new story line, I immediately weigh the idea next to these four standards I've set for myself.

The first word is *provocative.* When a reader picks up one of my books, I want her to think, to laugh, to cry, and in some cases, to remember a story long after she's put it down. Mostly, I want her to feel. My goal as a writer is to give my readers more than just a story; any writer worth their salt can do that. I want my stories to have layers to them — meaning, depth — so I work to provoke readers' thoughts.

The second word is *relevant.* All of my stories have to have some relevance to the readers who plunk down their hard-earned cash to read them. Readers need to identify with the characters on a personal level. Again, this is part of being a "value-added author," as I prefer to think of myself. My goal is to hit my readers right between the eyes. When I receive mail from readers who say they feel as if I've written about their lives, then I know I've achieved my goal.

The third criteria I set is to be *creative*. I challenge myself to think outside the box, to come up with an idea of presenting a tried-and-true story in a way that is fresh and different. I don't want to just scratch the surface — I want to get at the meat and the bones of an idea and make something that's provocative, that's relevant and created in a way that stays with my readers for a long time.

The last word I use as a measuring stick for my stories is *honesty*. I have to write from my heart. I have to be honest with myself and my readers, which means that my characters are flawed because I'm flawed. My characters face consequences to their actions because that's a universal law. There are good and bad consequences to our actions, and I refuse to hide them. Like Popeye, I am who I am, and I can't put on false pretenses even when it comes to characters and story.

Let me give you an example. One of my books, *Changing Habits,* which came out in 2003, is the story of three women who feel the call of God and enter a convent as Catholic nuns. The book chronicles their experiences in four parts: first, the call into religious life; second, their experiences in the novitiate; third, their years as professed sisters, the crisis of faith that leads to the decision to leave; and then, last, what happens to them as they leave and then struggle to make the transition from nuns to secular women.

The idea for *Changing Habits* came to me because of my cousin Shirley and her experience leaving the convent. On her birthday one year, I was with her and several of her friends. Shirley's friends were a hoot and so incredibly witty. I found myself laughing so hard my sides hurt, and that's when it hit me. I was the only woman there who had never been a nun. Each one of these women throbbed with story. I didn't know of anyone who had written a fictional book about life inside a convent or what happened to women who decided to leave.

I realized right away that this was an untapped story idea that would be provocative. It was certainly relevant to the times. I also knew that if I was going to write this story, I wanted to do it in a creative and engaging way that put the reader, Catholic or not, inside convent walls.

Probably the hardest part of creating this plot was being willing to be honest. I couldn't sugarcoat this story. I had to tell what I knew to be the truth. I knew that wouldn't be easy, especially since there was the risk I could offend my cousin and her friends. When it came right down to it, Shirley's friends didn't want me to write the book. They were afraid. One of my first tasks was to assure those I'd interviewed that it wasn't my intent to lambaste the church or use this book as a vehicle to ridicule them or the choices they'd made. But at the same time, I recognized that I had to be honest in the portrayal of the facts.

Now, you're probably wondering, *What does all this have to do with reading the Bible?* These words that guide my writing also come from reading my Bible. God's Word is definitely relevant; every single day, I come away with something God's shown me from reading His Word. It's provocative. There aren't many parts of it that you can gloss over without being forced to think about what you're reading and, as a result, what you're learning. The Bible is certainly honest — "In the beginning was the Word, and the Word was with God, and the Word was God" (John 1:1 NIV) — and from Genesis to Revelation it breathes creativity fashioned from our Creator. How awesome it is to know that my creativity comes from God!

The Discipline of Studying God's Word

It's not enough just to read God's Word; we must study it and commit it to memory. The more we have God's truth internalized, the better we can hear, understand, and *recognize* His voice giving us direction for our lives.

That's why learning to be disciplined and taking time to read God's Word each day is so important. Now, there's a difference between being disciplined and being legalistic. I like how dictionary.com defines *legalism:* "strict adherence to the letter . . . rather than the spirit." That's how so many of us approach our time with God every day — it's to the letter, it's by rote, it's mechanical; it's something we check off our list of 101 things to do for the day. If that's the case, then we're not coming with the right spirit. We're not approaching God's Word hungry and excited for what we're about to learn.

Martin Luther wrote:

I study my Bible like I gather apples. First, I shake the whole tree that the ripest may fall. Then I shake each limb, and when I

Knitting on the Word

Let's say I have just started learning how to knit. Chances are good that I've got knitting instructions right beside me every time I pull out a pair of knitting needles. Every step I come to, I go back and look at the instructions. I make the correct number of stitches. I follow the pattern until it is time to decrease for the shoulders, and then I measure and look to the pattern again. Back and forth I go, and the time it takes to do one row of stitches can be excruciatingly long.

What if I pick up that knitting only once a month? Maybe once every couple of months? How long do you think it might take until I can do it without the instructions? Six months? A year? Never? Unless I do it often enough so that it becomes an automatic action for me, I will never get there. I won't progress as a knitter, and I will stay a beginner. I'll never improve.

It's the same way with studying our Bible. We will never grow if we don't spend time committing its instructions to memory and taking its words to heart and acting on them.

have shaken each limb, I shake each branch and every twig. Then I look under every leaf. I search the Bible as a whole like shaking the whole tree. Then I shake every limb — study book after book. Then I shake every branch, giving attention to the chapters. Then I shake every twig, or a careful study of the paragraphs and sentences and words and their meanings.[4]

We need to be disciplined when it comes to reading God's Word. Discipline can help improve or develop us. It's a mental and spiritual practice of being in tune with God.

I've heard it said that there are two kinds of people in this world: the kind who get up in the morning and say, "Good morning, God," and the kind who get up and say, "Good God, morning."

I have to admit — I'm one of those disgusting morning people who wake up cheerful and ready to rip into my day. I was like this even before I was a writer; for me, morning is the best time to organize my thoughts, to journal, and to generate the energy I need to get things done.

I like to sit at our breakfast nook and watch the sun rise over the Cascade Mountains. It's an incredible sight when the sun bends down to kiss the earth. I have a stack of books I read from each morning: my Bible, several devotionals, and three journals. The three journals include my main journal, a gratitude journal, and a new one I've started where I write down the clever things my grandchildren say, or something funny that happens or that I hear about or wise sayings I find in my readings.

If anyone were to ask me what the one thing is that I do for myself that keeps me on track, I would definitely say it is the time that I reserve every morning for God and me. Notice the word I just used. I *reserve* that hour and a half. I make time for it, the same way I would a necessary medical procedure. I need that ninety minutes to feed myself spiritually and emotionally. Then, and only then, can I sit down and write from my heart.

> If any of you lacks wisdom, he should ask God, who gives generously to all without finding fault, and it will be given to him. (JAMES 1:5 NIV)

It never fails to surprise me how something in my daily reading will apply to the exact situation I'm dealing with at the time. Just recently I was in the book of Daniel. Most of us are familiar with the incredible story of Daniel in the lions' den, and he and his three friends who were thrown into the furnace. What I came away with from this reading — and I know I've read the entire book at least six times — was amazement at Daniel's integrity. As far as I can see, he remained faithful his entire life. Completely and utterly faithful. I want to be a Daniel. Debbie the Faithful. Debbie the Trusting.

Charles Swindoll, one of my favorite Christian writers, states:

Generally speaking, there are two kinds of tests in life; adversity and prosperity. Of the two, the latter is the more difficult. When adversity strikes, things get simple; survival is the goal. It is a test on maintaining the basics of food, clothing and shelter. But when prosperity comes, watch out! Things get complicated. All kinds of subtle temptations arrive, pleading for satisfaction. It is then that one's integrity is put to the test.[5]

It's tempting to put down the Word when things are going well. We see God's Word as a survival manual, to open only in an emergency. But when things are going great, when we're successful and prosperous and life is good, we fool ourselves into thinking that we don't need the Bible on a daily basis. We need to understand that the Bible isn't a parachute to prevent us from free-falling; it's the how-to guide that can keep us from falling in the first place.

Something else that helps me in my Bible reading and study is the dictionary I keep beside my Bible. I like to choose a few verses from each passage that I read and write them out; I find there is something about writing out the verses that helps better imprint their spiritual truths on my mind. After I've written out a verse, I pick out three or four words in that verse, and I go to the dictionary. It's also helpful to look at other Bible versions. I can't tell you how many different versions I have; there must be at least twenty Bibles at our house, but I love having them there to study. I look at each word in context, and I seek out the meaning behind the words. That's how I learn. That's how I grow.

Similarly, when it comes to learning about knitting, in addition to the skeins and skeins of yarn I have, I also own a lot of books on knitting. I like to read about knitting. There's one blog I read that's written by a knitter who calls herself the Yarn Harlot (YarnHarlot.com). You could call me that, too! She writes some of the funniest stuff. But ultimately, knitting is like playing the piano or writing: you won't learn to become an accomplished knitter unless you do it. The more we knit, the more beautiful the result can be. It's the same way with studying God's Word. The more we study and put God's Word into our hearts and lives, the more beautifully His love is able to be revealed through our actions.

I'm always amazed at the people I meet who have been knitting for years yet they only knit scarves. They don't have the self-confidence to knit anything more complicated. A scarf is all they are willing to try. What they don't realize is that every knitting project builds on the same basic stitches. They're comfortable knitting only one thing, and they stick with it instead of adding a new project to their repertoire. They get uneasy and are unwilling to attempt anything else, and yet, there are an endless number of other things available. Without even realizing it, they're missing out on so much fun and excitement. The resources are available, but they choose to miss out.

If only we could remember to go back to the Book when life gets complicated. That's why Bible study and consistent Bible reading are so important. Not to perform your Christian duty, not to check off a box that makes you feel better, but for the sole purpose of keeping your relationship with God strong.

Developing an Active Prayer Life

Besides writing out Scripture verses in my journal, I also like to write out my prayers. Putting my prayers down in word form has always been a wonderful way for me to communicate with God and write from my heart about what's concerning me. I love going back and reading the many journals I've saved from over the years and seeing how God has answered those prayers. That has really helped me develop my prayer life.

My daughter Jenny recently showed me a picture of my grandson Cameron, who is nine. Currently, Cameron's life ambition is to be an army general. This summer he spent quite a bit of time in his brother's sandbox, lining up and arranging little green army men in strategic battleground formations. He was so proud of his accomplishment that he insisted his mother take a photograph of his work on the off chance Jenny ran into someone from the army. She had his permission to pass along the photograph in case the army wanted to use his battle strategy. Jenny had the photograph with her when we flew into New York for a visit.

As it happens, my friend June Scobee Rodgers is married to a retired three-star general. Jenny shared Cameron's picture with Don, and the good man that he is, Don Rodgers wrote Cam a letter praising his efforts and asked for Cam's permission to share the battle plan with his friends at the Pentagon.

As I was looking at this picture, I realized that my prayers are much like those little green army men. It was a great reminder that my ways are not God's ways. His plans won't necessarily gel with the way I would like things to work out. Thankfully, God has left a number of my prayers unanswered and with good reason. God has the overall picture. After all, He's my General.

SAVORING GOD'S WORD

It's not enough to be disciplined to study; we need to take time to savor, to enjoy what God reveals to us through His Word. I love to spend time in my kitchen cooking up fabulous recipes for my family. One of the things I enjoy doing the most is going out to a restaurant, having an incredible meal, and then coming home and figuring out how I can replicate it. I think it's that way with God's Word, too. We can take the instruction and direction we read and figure out how to apply it to our day-to-day situations.

Did you know that God savors His time with us? He loves spending time with us; He delights in us. "The LORD delights in those who fear him, who put their hope in his unfailing love" (Psalm 147:11 NIV). He loves me so much, in fact, that He's going to give me a new name; not Debbie, but Sweetheart. A name of affection and love (Revelation 2:17).

One of the greatest ways I've found to savor His love and take to heart the lessons found in His Word is to study it with others. I've done many Bible studies through my church and with other ladies, and the benefits are enormous. Not only is there accountability, but there is joy in sharing and learning that comes from discussing what I'm reading with others. I've done Kay Arthur's Precepts studies, and those are excellent. I became rooted in the Word in five years of Bible Study Fellowship, too. Don't discount either your Sunday morning Sunday school or Bible study times.

The best way to learn God's Word is to teach it. I've prepared many Sunday school lessons for nearly every age-group from two-year-olds all the way through to junior high schoolers, and God has brought those lessons home to my heart as well.

Let me end this chapter with a story about the heart. Two years ago, after my father's death, I felt completely overwhelmed with life. Everything, it seemed, had fallen into my hands to take care of. My brother lived in Kansas, a thousand miles away, and though he called often, I was the one to help Mom make this huge adjustment in her life. The legal and financial matters were sometimes overwhelming.

Just when I thought I couldn't handle one more thing, Seattle underwent a cold snap that sent temperatures plummeting. Predictably, our heat pump chose to die that week. Wayne was out of town, so I was left to deal with that problem, too. It was just one more thing on top of everything else.

I called the repairman, who couldn't come for two days. I was left to parade through the house in my coat and gloves in an effort to keep warm. By the time the repairman arrived at my door, I was ready to pay anything to get that heat going again. I showed him where the furnace was and waited for his prognosis. To my surprise, he was back five minutes later, carrying two filters.

"Here's what's wrong," he said. "Your filters are dirty. Run these through your dishwasher and everything should be working as good as new." He left, and I couldn't help but laugh. The only thing wrong was plugged filters? That's what had kept me feeling like an icicle for two days?

As I set those filters in the dishwasher to clean, it hit me that they weren't the only things in need of a good wash. I needed some heart cleanup myself. I'd been carting around burdens, letting resentments build instead of giving them to the Lord. They were blocking my relationship with God and clouding my perspective.

I closed my eyes right then and there and asked for God's forgiveness. Later, as I replaced the cleaned filters, tears were in my eyes as the heat swirled through the vent, warming me . . . body and soul.

If you are in need of a heart cleanup, the best place to start is with the Word. Take the time you need to spend with God each day. Study His Word and memorize it so you can take it with you wherever you go. Savor His love for you, and remember that you are indeed created for the Word. It is

our only true road map that will show us
where to go next.

■ ■ ■ ■

8

CREATED FOR WORK

■ ■ ■ ■

I praise you because I am fearfully and
    wonderfully made;
your works are wonderful,
I know that full well.

PSALM 139:14 (NIV)

> The reward of a thing well done, is to
> have done it.
> RALPH WALDO EMERSON

When we start giving our dreams serious consideration, we often don't think about the work that's required to get us there. We look at successful people — CEOs of large companies, celebrities, sports figures — and we marvel at their successes. What we sometimes fail to see is how hard these folks worked to get where they are.

A glossy magazine cover of a Fortune 500 executive or a Billboard Top 40 recording artist shows us the glitz and the glamour, but it certainly doesn't tell the story behind the bright lights, big smiles, and carefully coiffed hair. We don't recognize the sweat, the pain, and the years it took to reach that level of success. We forget about the discipline and determination that person has maintained in order to keep his or her dream going. But I can assure you, it's there.

Think about the effort and the work God put into creating the world. For six days, He created and organized the planets, the oceans and land, the animals and the vegetation. The world was His dream, and He saw a purpose to it. His works are wonderful (Psalm 139:14), and we can see them all around us if we just look. He had a plan for the world and when we look at His works, we can be reminded of how important it is for us to do our own work in order to follow the plan He has for each of us.

After I sold my first book, I was like a lemming racing toward a cliff in my eagerness to write and sell as many books as quickly as possible. It wasn't until four or five years later that I realized how important it was for me to plan my work and work my plan; I discovered that if I was ever going to achieve lasting success in the writing world, I needed to work hard, and, more important, work smart. I needed a strategy.

SETTING GOALS

My first step, of course, was to look at God's Word, where there are actually a lot of verses about work. Genesis talks about the work God did creating the earth and how He rested on the seventh day (2:2), and Deuteronomy records how God blessed the work of Moses' hands (2:7). The search I did turned up more than 538 verses that mention the word *work* in the Bible. Clearly, work is an important part of life, not just now, but back in biblical times as well. But did you know that goals are also talked about in God's Word?

I press on toward the goal to win the prize for which God has called me heavenward in Christ Jesus. (PHILIPPIANS 3:14 NIV)

So we make it our goal to please him . . . (2 CORINTHIANS 5:9 NIV)

And on the third day I will reach my goal. (LUKE 13:32 NIV)

That last verse is Jesus Himself talking about goals. You see, when Jesus walked upon the earth, He set His course toward Calvary. Everything He said and did led Him in that direction. The Lord wants our lives to have direction, too.

When talking about being created for work, it is natural for me to discuss goals. Goals help us carry out the work. Too many of us sit back and wait for God to make everything happen, as if we're puppets, completely dependent on our master puppeteer to cause us to move. But that's not how God works, and that isn't how we should work, either.

WHY WE NEED GOALS

Goals are tremendously important to me. I've written them down for years, though they didn't always have my immediate attention. When I first started working with goals, I jotted down a couple of ambiguous ones and filed them away in the pages of my Bible. This was my way of letting God know what I wanted and that I was serious. In retrospect, I find that rather amusing.

If you've discounted the need for goals in the past, I hope you'll read the next few pages carefully, because goal setting is one of the most valuable career tools we can utilize to achieve success.

Goals give us somewhere to set our sights. Goals are like target practice — we get ready, we aim for what we want, and we fire away! Goals are not just the destination we're driving toward, they're also the painted white lines that keep us on the road.[1] By focusing on our goals, we stay centered on what's important and are better able to sort out the distractions that try to slow us down. I have to admit, I've learned this the hard way.

Because I love to knit, for my fiftieth birthday gift to myself, I attended a knitting conference in Pennsylvania, even though I was in the middle of writing a book and trying to meet my publisher's deadline. Many times when I attend a conference, it's to speak or lead a workshop, so I stay busy talking with people. One advantage of this is that I get to meet a lot of fans of my books. It was wonderful to be at this conference completely incognito. I bought enough yarn to clothe a third-world country and schmoozed with all the big names in the knitting world. At the banquet one night, a lady asked me if I ever got confused with the writer Debbie Macomber, and I assured her it happened all the time.

After I was home, it took me weeks to regain my momentum with the book I was writing. I ended up having to make more revisions on that book than I'd had to do in a long while.

The lesson I learned from this was the importance of maintaining my focus on whatever I'm doing, whether it's writing or anything else in my life. Goals help me do that.

There's a difference between deciding on a purpose and deciding on a goal. A purpose can be nebulous, but it crystallizes when you put goals with it, because goals have teeth. There's energy and action behind goals. When we establish goals, we impact our whole future. You may be reading this book feeling that your present circumstances are pretty bleak, but if you're willing to set positive, proactive goals for yourself, you'll take a big step toward improving your life.

When we focus our thoughts on a specific goal, something wonderful and magical occurs. Our minds start churning, finding ways to help us achieve our dreams. Now, understand what I'm saying and what I'm not saying. We can be positive without falling into the New Age philosophy that says I can think positively about anything and it will happen because I'm thinking positively. Philippians 4:13 tells us that we can do all things through Christ, who strengthens us. We can believe all things are possible with God's help — without saying, "All things are possible if I will it to be." As my friend Zig Ziglar says, "Positive thinking won't let you do anything, but it will let you do everything better than negative thinking will."[2]

So many of us, and I include myself here, are afraid of goals. We're afraid that if we aim too high, we'll only end up disappointed and disillusioned. We're afraid of failure, of the emotional consequences of defeat. There are enough negatives in life without setting ourselves up for more. Hey, I've been there and done that.

One of the things I think holds us back the most when it comes to goals is that deep down inside, most of us, despite what God tells us, don't think we deserve success. We see all of our faults and none of our value, especially the value God places on us. We hold all of our mistakes high and let our achievements fall by the wayside. We assume God sees us that way, too, and so we balk at the idea of setting goals.

When my son Ted was eight years old, he had a spiritual awakening. It was at a time when I was struggling; our church was in the midst of all kinds of problems, and I felt right in the middle. One day Ted and Steve, his friend from next door, were going to go ride their bikes outside.

They'd been gone only a few minutes when Ted burst back through the door, breathless with excitement. He and Steve had tried to get the bike out of Steve's garage, but the garage door wouldn't open. Ted had stopped what he was doing, quietly prayed that God would help open the garage door, and sure enough, the garage door opened. Ted was so excited.

"God answered my prayer, Mom," he said. "I'm going to be a missionary for Jesus!"

"That's wonderful, Ted," I said, somewhat absentmindedly. "Go only as far as darkest Africa and make sure you're home by dinnertime."

An hour or two passed and Wayne came home from work.

"Hey, sweetheart, have you seen Ted lately?" my husband wanted to know.

"He's out riding his bike with Steve," I said.

"No, Debbie," he said, smiling from ear to ear. "He's out on the corner, preaching."

I walked outside to call Ted in for dinner, and sure enough, there my little boy stood, on the corner of our street preaching to any car that passed. On the sidewalk near his feet, he had written in large chalk letters "Jesus Loves You. Ask Ted."

That night at bedtime, Ted crawled into my lap and looked into my face, a serious expression on his.

"Mom, I'm the one who lost Dad's hammer in the woods. I stole cookies out of the cookie jar, and I read Jody's journal."

I asked him why he was telling me all of this.

"Mom, I can't be a missionary for Jesus if I'm a bad sinner."

That conversation between this sweet little boy and his mother was such a valuable spiritual lesson for me about how God feels when we come to Him. His heart is as tender toward me as mine was toward Ted. When Ted confessed his sins, I had no thought of punishment or retribution, but only joy that he had come to me with a repentant heart.

God wants the best for us, and one of the ways we achieve the best is by setting goals to accomplish the work God has for us. He wants us to come to Him, just as Ted came to me, admitting our failures and ready to take on new challenges. As Eleanor Roosevelt said, "You must do the things you think you cannot do."

Remember those five goals I mentioned back in the very first chapter, goals I thought I would never be able to achieve? They were: (1) Consistent placement on the *New York Times* best-seller list; (2) books sold in audio format; (3) author tours; (4) movie deals; and (5) ABA (American Booksellers

Association) appearances. Shortly after finding those goals I'd written out several years earlier, I led a workshop with the board members for my local Romance Writers of America chapter and had five or six writers do this same exercise on bright pink recipe cards, writing down five goals that seemed beyond their wildest dreams.

I've kept up with those ladies since then, and all of them have achieved at least one of the goals on their lists. And while my own original five goals have all been fulfilled, I still carry a bright pink card with me — of new goals, just waiting to happen.

Now it's your turn. Overcome your fears today and grab an index card. Think about your dreams. Write down five things that seem beyond your wildest expectations. Keep this card with you. Refer to your list often, using it as a checkpoint. It will keep you on track and help you avoid unnecessary detours.

Let me make one last point about managing our fears when it comes to goals. In the movie *Hoosiers,* Gene Hackman plays the part of Norman Dale, a former college coach with a tainted past who is hired to coach a rural high-school basketball team from Hickory, Indiana. Coach Dale leads the team all the way to the state finals. On the day of the semifinals, the team arrives at Butler Field House, the huge inner-city arena where they will play in just a couple of hours. When the players enter the arena, their jaws fall slack and their eyes open wide. Gawking at the seats, the stand-alone goals, the suspended scoreboard, and the lights, they are awestruck and intimidated.

Coach Dale instructs one of his players to take a tape measure and determine the distance between the free-throw line and the goal.

"What's the distance?" he asks.

"Fifteen feet," the player says.

The coach then tells the smallest player on the team to climb on the shoulders of a taller player so they can measure the goal. "How high is it?" he asks.

"Ten feet," the player says.

Coach Dale says, "I believe you'll find these are the exact same measurements as our gym back in Hickory."

Sometimes when we're shooting for the top, it feels as though we're shooting for the moon. Keep your goals in perspective, and realize that quite often the obstacles are not nearly as large as we perceive them to be.

Knowing who we are and what we want to accomplish is vital as we determine our goals. I accepted a long time ago that the books I write probably aren't going to change the world. I'll leave that up to people with a much larger vocabulary than mine. However, I consider it my duty, indeed, my responsibility, to touch my readers' emotions. A reader's problems won't go away because she's read my books, but my goal is for her to feel better about life because through my stories she's met characters like herself who faced trouble with both courage and honor. I want to change her world for the better through the power of love. My goal is for a reader to finish my book feeling positive and hopeful about solving her own problems. That driving goal makes me proud to write my books.

Once I established that goal in written form, I was able to set each story line up against it to see if I had hit the mark. As my books sold successfully and my readers increased in number, I was able to look at my written goal and understand what it was about my books that people loved. I know myself and I know my goals.

Goals give me a target to shoot for. If I know what I want, then I can figure out how to get there. I have weekly goals that I set the first of each week, and daily ones, too. Once a year, usually in January, I take an entire day with my husband and set goals in a variety of areas that we do on a goal worksheet I developed several years ago. It sounds like a lot of work, and it is, but it has proved to be an invaluable aid over time. For a number of years my children and I sat down and did the worksheet together. I would encourage you to look at the sample we've included here at the end of the chapter and include your family in this exercise.

This year I set seventy-two achievable goals for myself, divided among eight categories that include: Physical, Mental, Spiritual, Recreational, Family Centered, Career Centered, Social, and Financial. At the beginning of every month, I review these eight categories to see how I'm doing. If I find myself falling short in one area, then I stop and analyze what I can do to improve and then mentally start working on getting back on course. Take a look at the example of a goal worksheet to help you get started with your own goals.

There are a few things I keep in mind when I sit down to plan out my goals. First, I'm very specific. I don't say, "I'd like to sell some books this year." One of the first goals I ever made was to write three books in one year. Write and *sell.* That's specific.

I'm also realistic. Notice that I said I set *achievable* goals for myself. Why set goals that are impossible to achieve? That only encourages us *not* to set goals, because we never see success. So the goals I set are achievable. They're reachable.

I do have another category for goals I have no control over. I call it my "Some Things Have to Be Believed before They Can Be Seen" category. I saw that statement on a billboard one time and it stuck with me. There are some goals — I call them "gutsy goals" — that I have absolutely no control over. I have no say in whether my book reaches number one on the *New York Times* best-seller list. I can write a book I think is worthy, but I have no control over its sales or reviews or recognitions. Those types of goals are out of my hands, but it doesn't mean I can't wish for them.

At the age of fifteen, John Stoddard made a list of all the things he wanted to accomplish in his life. He envisioned himself as a great explorer and listed things like: explore the Nile; climb Mount Everest; visit every country in the world; visit the moon. His list had 127 goals.

By the time John was sixty years old, he had become an author and lecturer and made many explorations. He often smiled when asked about the list he'd made so many years earlier. He said, "Nearly everyone has goals and dreams, but not everyone acts on them. There are things on the list I will never do: Star in a Tarzan movie or climb Mount Everest. Goal setting is like that. Some may be beyond your reach, but you don't have to give up on the dream."[3]

So there are achievable goals, goals you can work hard for and accomplish. And then there are gutsy goals; dreams you have to believe in and hope for. All of these can be included in your goal worksheet.

When setting goals, it's also important to be aggressive. Here's what I mean by that: when I set goals, I make sure they're realistic but that doesn't mean they're easy. If I set only easy ones that I could complete in the first half of a given year, what would I do for the last half?

I like to set both short-term and long-term goals, some simple, some more complicated. One of my goals this next year is to plan a trip to cruise around the Hawaiian Islands with my entire family. Fulfilling that goal is just a matter of scheduling time to contact the travel agent and coordinate everyone's

Knitting on Work

"With a little practice and patience, our hands learn to knit; then our minds are free to enjoy the process."
— Bev Galeskas, Fiber Trends

When we use goals to help us with our work, we actually create a pattern, much like what we use in knitting. I know there are knitters out there who can sit down without a pattern and create beautiful garments, but for me, starting with a pattern, a plan, in place is so much easier.

Keep in mind that working with patterns, or within the framework of goals, doesn't mean you're working in a box. I know many women — and men, too — who will start a knitting project with a pattern and then use their own creativity to make that pattern their own. It's the same way with our goals and our work. Start with a plan and then let God add creative and wonderful enhancements that make those plans even better. I knit every day; it's important to keep going. It's the same with our work.

schedules. That's short-term. It doesn't take all year to do that. Another goal might be working with my publicist on a new Web site design. That will take time to develop, and there will be several steps to complete for that one goal. That's long-term.

One last point to think about when setting goals is to make sure they are consistent and don't conflict with one another. If one of my goals is to travel around the world for a year, that might make it hard to fulfill my other goal of developing better relationships with the ladies in my Sunday school class.

Think long and hard about the direction you're taking when deciding on what you're doing and what you're not doing. Goals are a tool just as serious as your computer or your accountant's advice.

ACHIEVING YOUR GOALS

Once we've set our goals, there are still things we can do to make sure we achieve them. Whether we work full-time outside the home, work at home, work part-time, or whatever our day-to-day schedule consists of, it's important that we're working toward, not away from, the things we're trying to accomplish.

Billy Graham once said, "The greatest waste in all of our earth, which cannot be recycled or reclaimed, is our waste of the time that God has given us each day."[4]

I follow a schedule, and I definitely recommend that you try doing the same. On weekdays, I typically wake up at 4:00 a.m. and take time to read my Bible and write in my journals. Then I go to the local high school and swim half a mile. By 8:00 a.m., I'm in my office, where I read and answer my mail and e-mail. Around 10:00 a.m., I start writing. I have a daily goal for writing a certain number of pages. I don't leave the office until I'm finished. I generally tend to stay until 4:00 or 5:00 p.m. Once I'm home, my time and attention are devoted to my husband and any other family who happen to be over. I'm usually heading toward bed by nine and asleep by ten. Since Wednesday is my administrative day and I can sleep in later on Saturdays, sometimes I'll stay up a little later on Tuesday nights and Friday nights, too.

Schedules are helpful because they give you a consistent and constant rhythm. But what works for me may not work for you. My schedule has also changed a bit over the years as my children have grown and established their own lives. Years ago I still got up early to do Bible study, but those morning hours also included getting lunches ready, getting Wayne out the door and ready for his day as an electrician, and making sure the kids had what they needed for their school day.

You will have your own unique schedule, depending on your situation and responsibilities. Take a few minutes to sit down and sketch out the kind of schedule that will work for you. How would you describe your typical day? Make a list of everything you usually do during a given day. Be honest with yourself. Include the things you may do that are time-wasters, like watching that favorite soap opera, or playing computer games, or checking e-mail more than five times a day. Now go back and look at your day's schedule. Are there things you can cut out? Things you can combine?

It's okay to schedule downtime, or fun time; just make sure it's helping and not taking away from what you're trying to accomplish. What else should you consider adding to your schedule to help you achieve your goals?

Develop a schedule that works for you and your family, and try to follow it to the best of your ability, but take a warning from someone who knows: resist putting it into concrete. Think of it more as plastic sheeting. Concrete cracks and breaks, but plastic sheeting is flexible. Be flexible. Emergencies will come up; kids will get sick, plans will change. Don't become discouraged when the schedule seems to get thrown out the window one day. At the same time, don't let that one day become one week or even longer. The sooner you can develop a set schedule, the easier it will be to follow, and the easier it will be to accomplish your goals.

I talked about time-wasters earlier: let's go over some time-savers we can use to keep us on schedule and effectively using our time.

Time-Saver Tip #1

Be willing to get rid of things. Take a blank 5×7 card and write the following: *Hello, my name is (fill in the blank) and I throw things away.*

Time-Saver Tip #2

Organize your mail as you're going through it. Whenever I open my mail, I follow what is known as the RAFT system. I call it RAFT because if I follow it, then I've set a course for smooth sailing.

R stands for Refer, a way of delegating the mail. This simply means if I open a bill, I stick it in the bill envelope I take to the accountant. Letters go to my assistant to answer with my instructions.

A stands for Action. If a letter is requesting something that needs to be done that day, I don't put it off. I do it then.

F stands for File. But be strategic in what you stick in that manila folder because 80 percent of what we file we never look at again. Before you file, ask yourself: Will I need this in the next month? Will I need this in the next six months? If you can't honestly say yes, then it's time to look at the last letter of RAFT.

T stands for Toss. I have a large garbage can that sets directly beside my desk, and I don't think twice about using it.

Time-Saver Tip #3

Read your mail with a highlighter. I recently learned of this tip, and I can tell you, I have already discovered its advantages. Underline what you need to remember before you set it aside, and then when you reach for it later, you'll know at a glance what's expected of you without having to reread the entire letter.

Time-Saver Tip #4

Don't do today what you can put off until tomorrow. I took a time management class a year ago that suggested buying forty-three file folders. The first thirty-one are numbered for the days of the month. The next twelve are months of the year. If you open a bill on the sixth that's due to be paid by the thirtieth, slip it into the file for the twenty-third and pay it then. I've used this system at other times in my life and can testify that it works wonderfully well.

Time-Saver Tip #5

Avoid the magazine mayhem. For years I've subscribed to a number of magazines. My husband and I routinely receive close to thirty magazines a month. I had no idea it was so many until it came time for us to move and I had to put in the change of address forms. The magazines stack up and frustrate and overwhelm me. I've devised a system, though, that works well for me. When a magazine first arrives, I go through it, decide which of the articles are of interest to me, and tear them out, stapling the pages together and placing them inside a manila file folder. When I have a spare minute, I grab one of those articles and read it. This eliminates wasted time. Because I've already decided what articles are of interest to me, I don't have to flip through the magazine a second time, or even pick it up more than once. At the end of the month, I review the articles I have left and decide whether I really want to read them or not.

Time-Saver Tip #6
Stay organized. Neatness counts. Organize your work space and make sure you have everything you need before starting a project. When you're finished with something, put it away. Don't leave anything lying out.

Time-Saver Tip #7
Think about tomorrow before you leave today. Before you stop work, make a list of your priorities for the following day. You'll sleep more soundly if you're not worried about forgetting to do something in the morning. Arrive early to work and give yourself ten or fifteen minutes to review the list you wrote the night before. It sets your priorities in your mind and gets you working toward achieving those priorities.

One of the best ways to reach our goals is to have others hold us accountable. We all need accountability partners — in work and in life. I find great accountability with my Breakfast Club friends, my husband, and those friends who I know are encouragers.

After listening to Zig Ziglar and Brian Tracy's audiotapes and other materials, I started getting offers from them to enroll in a course that came with a "success coach." I put it off several times, thinking it was too expensive and I was too busy. But in 1996, it dawned on me that my career wasn't ever going to get any less busy, so I signed up for Zig's seminar. It was one of the best business decisions I've ever made, and a lot of it has to do with the accountability I had through my success coach. She offered assignments, and it was up to me to complete them. If I didn't, I wasn't just letting myself down, I was letting her down, too.

Once you have your goals in place, give a copy of your goals to someone you trust, someone who will keep you accountable. Perhaps you can be accountable to each other. Schedule regular times to get together and review how each of you are doing with your goals. When you make the time to review your goals with someone else, you will have more incentive to closely examine what's working and what isn't.

Don't Be Afraid of the D-Word

I mentioned this in the chapter on success, but another great way to make sure you're on course to completing your goals is to delegate! Let's say that one of your goals under your Family category is to have dinner as a family at least three times a week. Ask your husband or an older son or daughter to help you with the grocery list. Take turns planning and cooking the meals, and definitely enlist help with the cleanup. Not only will you save time, but you'll also get your family working together, which will instill bigger lessons with your kids long-term than just cooking dinner together.

Many of us find a lot of excuses not to delegate, in work and in life. We think we can do something better than someone else, or we worry that we're adding to someone else's plate just to make ours lighter. We think we just don't have the time to show someone else how to do something — and on and on it goes.

Of course, not everything should be delegated. Don't delegate what you can eliminate. This goes back to what we talked about in chapter 4: there are just some things that you shouldn't be doing. Find those time-wasters and get rid of them. Don't pass them off to someone else. What we do want to pass on to others are routine activities. Delegation makes the most sense in a work setting, but it can also be used when you're involved in church activities or committees, or helping with your child's classroom at school.

WHEN WE MISS A GOAL

So what happens if we miss a goal? Do we scratch it off, never to visit it again? Do we hang our heads in shame, and beat ourselves up for failing? I sure hope not. If I'd done that, I'd have had a lot of black-and-blue marks over the years!

Remember when I talked about valuing the small successes along the way? We can take a similar approach when it comes to difficult goals. If I don't achieve a certain goal the first time, I've learned to break it up into smaller pieces and tackle those pieces one at a time.

Years ago, when I first started thinking about career planning, I began paying attention to best-seller lists. Each month I'd visit my local Walden Books store and check out the latest best-seller list. I remember the first time I saw the Walden list. At that point in my career, I was writing what are known as category romances. I must have had twenty books under my belt, but my name wasn't on "the list." I wanted to know why because I thought my books were great. (Remember, I'm a positive person, and humble too!)

So I quickly set a goal to make it onto the

Walden best-seller list. I started keeping track of the list and after a while, I noticed something that was a real eye-opener to me. Each book on the list shared a commonality — a strong title. I noticed certain key words showing up in the best-selling titles. Once I recognized that, I changed my own titles to a more romantic slant and started making the list on a regular basis.

Coming up short on a goal should be a signal to us to step back and examine that goal again. Turn it over; turn it around; look at what you could have done instead of what you did. Break the goal up into smaller pieces and tackle it again.

She sets about her work vigorously; her arms are strong for her tasks. (PROVERBS 31:17 NIV)

If goals are vital to do our work, then work is vital to fulfill our purpose. Don't be overwhelmed and feel that you need to set a huge number of goals your first time out of the goal-setting gate. Start with one or two that align with the dream you're trying to accomplish. Then do everything you can to reach those goals. And when you complete them, set more. Pretty soon, you'll find yourself truly enjoying the amazing journey

God has set you on!

Sample Worksheet:

GOALS FOR THIS YEAR

List three new things you'd like to experience this year:

1.
2.
3.

List three nonfiction books you want to read this year:

1.
2.
3.

List three things about yourself you want to improve:

1.
2.
3.

I. Spiritual goals

II. Family goals

III. Physical goals

IV. Career goals

V. Recreational goals

VI. Financial goals

■ ■ ■ ■

9
CREATED FOR LAUGHTER

■ ■ ■ ■

My frame was not hidden from you when I
  was made in the secret place.
When I was woven together in the depths
  of the earth.

PSALM 139:15 NIV

> What soap is to the body, laughter is to
> the soul.
>   YIDDISH PROVERB

Anyone who knows me knows I love to laugh. I love it so much that one of the journals I keep is a leather-bound book I call my Laughter Journal. I usually write down all of the funny things my grandkids say, or other jokes or humorous slices of life that happen from day to day. Funny, delightful moments I don't want to forget.

Like the last time I went and picked up my six-year-old granddaughter, Maddy, to come spend the night with me. Sitting in the backseat, she was muttering something under her breath, and I asked her to repeat what she said. With long-suffering patience, she explained: "Sorry, Grandma, that wasn't for adult ears." I had to write that down.

Or the recent trip to New York with my daughters: Saturday night in our hotel room, trying to get my panty hose on. Putting them on isn't a pretty sight. Maybe you can sympathize. They have to feel right, so I do these rather complicated stretching exercises and prance around the room like a high-stepping horse. Bend over, squat down — that sort of thing. When I found my daughters staring at me in utter befuddlement, I explained what I was doing and why. Then I added that I don't even let their father see me put on panty hose. Jody looked at me and said, "Gee, Mom, how did we get so lucky?" When we got back, that was the next entry in my journal, right after a quote I heard recently about Santa Claus and the stages of life:

You believe in Santa Claus.
You don't believe in Santa Claus.
You become Santa Claus.
You look like Santa Claus.

We were created for laughter, and I believe laughter is a central part of purpose, because our purpose is a journey — and what kind of journey would it be without laughter or joy? See if you can find what Psalm 139:11–12 says about laughter:

If I say, "Surely the darkness will hide me and the light become night around me," even the darkness will not be dark to you; the night will shine like the day, for darkness is as light to you. (NIV)

To me, laughter is a ray of sunshine that perks us up when we're down and keeps us going when we just want to stop. It is a way to bring light into the dark as we pursue our purpose. God does not dwell in darkness. He radiates light! He radiates joy!

I don't believe I've met one person in my lifetime who has told me they don't enjoy laughing. Everyone loves to laugh. It's just something that's built into us, this need to chuckle and giggle and titter and be jocular and merry. I come from a big, extended family, and laughter and joy and fun were always important parts of the Adler clan. It makes sense — studies show that people tend to laugh thirty times more when they're in a group.[1] I'm convinced that we can get through anything in life if we can laugh about it, and laugh with one another.

A LAUGH A DAY KEEPS THE DOCTOR AWAY

Laughter isn't just a good feeling; it can also be *good medicine.* It's good for our hearts and for our souls.

277

In *The Anatomy of an Illness as Perceived by the Patient,* Norman Cousins shares his story of being hospitalized with a rare, painful, and crippling disease back in the early 1970s. When he was told there was no cure, Norman checked himself out of the hospital, determined to find a cure himself. Knowing that negative emotions can be harmful to the body, Norman reasoned that the opposite must also be true. So he borrowed a movie projector and designed his own treatment, which included Marx Brothers films and old *Candid Camera* reruns. He soon discovered that ten minutes of laughter provided two hours of pain-free sleep. Eventually, his debilitating disease was cured, by all intents and purposes, through natural healing methods, and when his case was reported in the *New England Journal of Medicine,* Norman received more than three thousand letters from thankful doctors around the world.[2]

Norman's case triggered a series of studies and ongoing analysis of how laughter makes us healthier. Doctors and scientists already know that laughter reduces levels of certain stress hormones that are responsible for suppressing our immune systems and raising our blood pressure, among other things. They've also discovered that laughing one hundred times is equal in benefit to spending ten minutes on the rowing machine or fifteen minutes on an exercise bike. We're talking a total body workout! Blood pressure lowers, and an increase in vascular blood flow and oxygenation of the blood helps with additional healing. Laughter can also give our diaphragm, abdominal, respiratory, facial, leg, and back muscles a workout. That's why we often feel so tired after sharing a lot of laughs with friends; we've really just been to the gym![3]

Something else that researchers have pointed out is that positive and negative emotions can't be experienced simultaneously. We can't laugh and feel pain at the same time. Have you ever done something silly like bump your head when you stood up or lose your balance and fall for no real reason? At the moment it happened, the humor of the situation hit you quicker than the pain did, and chances are, while you were laughing, you didn't feel a thing. It was only after you stopped laughing that you felt the full impact of what just happened and the realization that there would be a bruise in the morning.

Lee Berk is the associate director of the Center for Neuroimmunology and an associate research professor of pathology and human anatomy at the School of Medicine at Loma Linda University in California. He and his colleagues have done many studies over the years that show laughter doesn't just benefit us for health reasons; it's a great way to help us feel good emotionally, too. "We seek humor and laughter because it feels good," Berk says. "It feels good because it's triggering the entire limbic system."[4]

Humor starts the activity in the brain necessary to help our blood flow increase and release positive hormones and endorphins. We feel more energy, and negative chemicals in our brain, like stress, are suppressed. Bottom line, laughter makes us feel good. Here's something else that's interesting, even when we're *not* in a funny mood, if we force ourselves to laugh, our bodies react the same way they would if we really had something funny to laugh about. So the next time you're in a bad mood, make yourself laugh and wait for those endorphins to kick in — you'll feel a lot better in no time.

Remember the movie *Patch Adams,* starring Robin Williams? It was about the story of the real-life Patch Adams, a doctor who didn't look, act, or think like a typical doctor. For Patch, humor was the best medicine for his patients, and in the movie, he showed that he was willing to do just about anything to make the patients laugh, even if it meant risking his own career. The real Patch Adams carries out his mission of healing with humor to this day through his Gesundheit! Institute. He and his team take their clowning trips all over the world, bringing smiles and laughs to children and adults alike. He encourages anyone in the medical field to make house calls and to look for fresh ways to bring a smile to someone who's not feeling well.

A nurse named Amanda shares on Patch's Web site that humor is an intricate part of how she helps her patients care for their spirits as well as their bodies. She writes: "My favorite thing that my patients say is, 'I hope all these pills know what they are supposed to do.' To which I cheerfully reply, 'Yeah, I hope they didn't give you the one that wants to be a stool softener instead of a blood pressure pill.' This always gets me a laugh."[5]

Even hospitals in Israel have taken the cue that laughter helps heal. Assaf Harofe Hospital in Tzrifin, near Tel Aviv, offers an eighty-hour, six-month course that teaches students the art of clowning. One of the pediatricians who started the course, Dr. Shai Pintov, says that research on patients has confirmed the notion that "laughter is the best medicine" and that clown therapy is a unique way to treat patients and speed their recovery time.[6]

Laughter also helps us deal with stress in a healthy way. The Pentagon has now started offering military families a laughter program as a way to help them cope with the stress of deployment. Retired U.S. Army Colonel James "Scotty" Scott went through laughter training with the Ohio-based World Laughter Tour, a group that promotes humor as a healthy solution. The group points to the studies that suggest laughter can boost the body's immune system and decrease stress hormones. Now Scotty takes his training and shares what he knows with military families and reservists. "The guiding principle is to laugh for no reason. And that's one of the reasons it works so well for military families," he says. "There's a lot they have to be stressed over; a lot of worries, a lot of concerns."[7]

NOT SO SERIOUS

So, if laughter makes us feel good, if it helps us cope with stress and keep our hearts healthy and our minds clear, why is it that as adults, we laugh so much less than we did as kids? While the numbers differ depending on the reports you read, it's clear that children laugh quite a bit more than adults on a daily basis. Where along life's way did we lose our sense of humor?

God ordains a good sense of humor. Read what His Word says about it:

A cheerful heart is good medicine, but a crushed spirit dries up the bones. (PROVERBS 17:22 NIV)

A happy heart makes the face cheerful, but heartache crushes the spirit. (PROVERBS 15:13 NIV)

We were created to have joy. We were created to enjoy laughter and share it with one another. I'm afraid that there are many Christians today who are afraid of having joy, but we were created for it. So many people want to be so serious. I remember sitting one day with my Bible in front of me, having a really hard time with the verse "And Jesus wept" (John 11:35 NIV). As a writer, the thought came to me that instead of saying that, I would have liked if God had said "And Jesus laughed." Of course, God's voice suddenly boomed in my heart — "Thou shalt not edit God!"

We were created to laugh. Over the years

I've received literally thousands of letters from my readers, and I treasure every one. Some, however, are more special than others. Let me share with you a selection of quotes from some of my favorites:

"You're my favorite writer. I'll buy anything that has your name on it. So, thank you, *Betty.*" This dear soul apparently likes my writing, but she's out there looking for books written by someone named *Betty!*

That's similar to something another lady wrote: "I just finished reading *Twice Loved.* It was the best book I ever read. Thank you for writing such a wonderful book." Oops, I didn't write that book. LaVyrle Spencer did!

One older lady has found a way to save those valuable book dollars. "I exchange books with friends, but get mine back because I reread them. Since I'm older, I can't remember what they were about."

I do think this reader meant this following comment as a compliment. "I love your books; they put me to sleep every night."

Another lady who wrote to me said, "I love your books so much I'm willing to pay for them." I do hope that doesn't mean she takes other books without paying for them. . . .

Knitting on Laughter

"In the hands of a knitter, yarn becomes the medium that binds the heart and soul." — Robin Villiers-Furze, The Needleworks Company of Port Orchard

It's always been my thought that if you can't laugh when you're knitting, you need to find something else that you enjoy doing! I have had more fun and more joy when I'm with a group of friends and we all have our knitting out. We talk and share stories and laugh together about old times or recent funny moments. Just like life, we can get too serious about our knitting and it can become work and the garments we make become chores. Let me encourage you to keep a good sense of humor — not only as you count stitches, but in your everyday life.

OLDER AND SIMPLER KNOW BEST

My older readers often worry that I'm not writing fast enough. Here are a couple of examples of the requests I receive:

"When is that next Cedar Cove book coming out? I'm 85 — hurry."

She isn't the only one who hates having to wait a year for the next in my hometown series. One lady wrote, "Please get going on the next Cedar Cove book. I made my friend promise that if I should die before next September, she'll visit my grave and read it to me."

As I mentioned earlier, I married soon after I graduated from high school and had four children in five years. It never bothered me that I missed a college education; I've been able to function quite well in this world and consider myself self-taught. I've never stopped reading, never stopped learning, but apparently my lack of college education is more obvious to some readers than I thought:

"I like you best because you use small words."

Of course there's the occasional letter that comes with an offer. One mother wrote, "You sound like such a nice person. You're just the kind of woman I'd like my son to marry. He's 52 and lives at home; are you interested?" I wrote her back and told her I had all I could handle with Wayne, who also happened to be fifty-two at the time.

I love hearing from my readers — the good letters as well as the bad. I'll never forget when a reader wrote to my editor to complain about my books. The letter was several pages long and single-spaced. She'd mention a title of mine and then list everything she felt was wrong with it. This went on for paragraph after paragraph. Finally, the very last sentence of the letter said, "In fact, I've read every one of Debbie Macomber's books and I haven't liked a one of them." Well, she may not like them, but she sure is a faithful reader!

LAUGHTER AND JOY, LIKE A GOOD BOOK, CAN HELP US COPE

George is a favorite reader of mine. He's in his eighties and is a real sweetheart. Several years ago he went through a bout of ill health and suffered from depression. One day, he picked up one of my traditional romances at a garage sale for five cents. His wife was reading something else at the time, so he decided to read the book himself. He soon found himself chuckling. He then went on a book search and found several more of my books, and surprise, surprise, unlike the woman with the three pages of complaints, he enjoyed them. That worried him enough that he made an appointment with his doctor. He was convinced there was something wrong and told the doctor that "this woman's books make me laugh." He wasn't sure he should be reading them because they were romances. The doctor told him to go ahead and read them but not to tell anyone.

And then there's the ever-popular prison mail, the source of my all-time favorite reader letter. I was so impressed with what one inmate had to say that I brought his letter home and waved it under Wayne's nose. This man wrote and told me, "You can be my woman and I don't even care if you're fat." I made sure I let my husband know that I could have this man any time I wanted.

A Texas prisoner once wrote: "You haven't got a thing to worry about if you write me. I haven't got a vicious bone in my body. As for the stabbing, the other guy asked for it."

Convicted felons aren't my only large following. Apparently there are a number of FBI agents who read my books, too. Because of an incident with one of my daughter's coworkers, Jody was interviewed by two FBI agents. She told me how stiff and unemotional the two women agents were as she answered their questions. Following the interview, one agent said she had a question that was completely voluntary — Jody didn't have to answer it if she didn't want to.

"Are you related to Debbie Macomber?"

When Jody explained that she was my daughter, the agent came unglued, threw her arms in the air, and told Jody that the FBI has its own Debbie Macomber fan club.

FINDING THE LAUGHTER IN LIFE

I share these letters and stories with you because I want you to know that I don't take myself too seriously and neither should you. There's a danger we have to watch out for when pursuing our dreams or our passions: we can get so serious, so focused, that we leave the joy and the laughter behind and our mission turns into living for the battle instead of living for life.

Best-selling author and radio communicator Dr. Charles Swindoll, in his book *Laugh Again,* writes about talking with a man who had been raised in an "ultra-serious" home where feelings weren't talked about and work was overemphasized. The man told Dr. Swindoll that it was ironic that in his sixty-plus years, he had achieved everything he dreamed of doing and had been rewarded for it. "My problem," the man said, "is that I don't know how to have fun and enjoy these things hard work has brought me. I cannot remember the last time I laughed — I mean, really laughed." As he turned to walk away, he said he probably needed to work harder at being happier. Charles reached over, touched the man's arm, and said: "Trust me on this one — a happy heart is not achieved by hard work and long hours. If it were, the happiest people on earth would be the workaholics . . . and I have never met a workaholic whose sense of humor balanced out his intensity."[8]

LEARNING HOW TO LAUGH AT OURSELVES

Probably the most well-known account of laughter in the Bible has to do with Abraham's wife, Sarah. She was ninety years old when God sent two angels to tell Abraham that his wife would have a child. Many point out that Sarah's laughter was a sign she didn't believe God.

> Then the LORD said to Abraham, "Why did Sarah laugh and say, 'Will I really have a child, now that I am old?' Is anything too hard for the LORD? I will return to you at the appointed time next year and Sarah will have a son." (GENESIS 18:13–14 NIV)

It's interesting to note, though, that

Abraham's reaction when God first told him that Sarah was to have a son was also one of laughter (Genesis 17:17). While we always want to trust what God tells us, I tend to think that part of Sarah's laughter wasn't disbelief, but was perhaps a little bit of laughing at herself. Look at what she says in Genesis 18:12: "So Sarah laughed to herself as she thought, 'After I am worn out and my master is old, will I now have this pleasure?' " (NIV). I like how *The Message* puts it: "An old woman like me? Get pregnant? With this old man of a husband?"

Can you imagine what was going through her head as she overheard these men tell her husband that she was going to have a baby? Do you think she stood there and looked down at her frail, weakening ninety-year-old body and just shook her head? Do you think she instantly thought of all the baby clothes and diapers she would be washing, the sleepless nights, the bouts of colic? I can just imagine what was going through her mind: *I can barely walk myself at my age; now I'm going to have to keep up with a toddler? Well, at least we'll both be tottering!*

No doubt, I would have had to laugh, too.

Over the course of my career, there have been lots of moments I've had the opportunity to have a good chuckle at my own expense.

God's Perfect Timing

The year my husband was living in Nevada was a tough one, and I was struggling, paycheck to paycheck. For no real reason, my friend Linda Miller and I decided that we were going to act like hotshot writers and fly to Boston to stay at the RWA Conference in a fabulous hotel. We booked a huge suite.

We had it all worked out. Each of us would bring a friend. The suite was two hundred dollars a night; we would each pay fifty dollars and it would be just perfect. But at the last minute, both of our friends canceled out on us and the hotel was sold out, so there was no way to request a regular room. The appointed time came and we flew from Seattle to Boston, with no idea how we were going to pay for this suite. Once we arrived at the hotel, I showed the clerk our reservation number and we nervously waited to get checked in. Only God knew how we were going to pay for this when the bill arrived. The clerk typed in our reservation number and then called the manager over. The manager repeated the process and then looked at Linda and me.

"Ladies, I'm so sorry, but somehow we gave your reservation away. We have another room, but it only has one bathroom, so we're only going to charge you fifty dollars a night." I can remember looking at Linda and both of us bursting into laughter. Once more God had taken care of us.

Seaplane Adventures

Linda and I have had lots of adventures together. Another one involved chartering a seaplane for the day. One of the books I was writing at the time had a seaplane in it, and I wanted to know what it would be like to fly in one, so for Linda's birthday I decided to charter one to fly us to a wonderful resort and spa in the San Juan Islands. We were looking forward to getting facials and manicures, but just as we were leaving to meet the seaplane, Wayne cautioned us when we climbed aboard.

"Be careful," he said. "The docks can be slippery."

Both of us took tiny, careful steps as we boarded the plane that morning. I climbed in back, and Linda successfully managed to get into the front seat. We were giving each other enthusiastic high fives for successfully making it into the plane when I heard a tremendous splash. Our pilot had fallen into the water! So there we sat, slowly floating into Sinclair Inlet in a plane with our pilot frantically swimming after us. Meanwhile, Linda and I were desperately trying to figure out how best to help him.

"Throw him your purse strap!"

"I'm not throwing him my purse strap! You throw him yours!"

Eventually, the pilot made it into the plane and we were on our way for a — very much-needed, by that point — afternoon at the spa.

"EVEN YOU!"

One of the bonuses of writing fiction has been all of the wonderful places I've traveled to over the years to do research for my books.

I remember the year I traveled to Hong Kong. I had a wonderful time exploring the sights and sounds of the area, and one afternoon I was standing in the middle of Stanley Market, which is possibly the most wonderful market in the world. As you know, Chinese women there are very tiny and petite, graceful and slender — qualities I wouldn't necessarily use to describe myself.

A small Asian woman jumped out from one of the stalls, stood in the middle of the aisle, and pointed directly at me and shouted:

"We've got sizes to fit even *you!*"

Someone later asked me if I was insulted, and I said not at all — until then I hadn't been able to find anything there large enough to fit over my big toe!

LESSONS IN ALASKA

On another research trip, my husband, Wayne, and I flew up to Alaska on a research expedition. I had lined up several interviews with bush pilots, and one of the pilots I talked with had a commuter air service. He offered to take us on a mail run.

Before we got into the tiny plane, the pilot asked for our weights. Wayne gave his easily enough, but then the pilot turned to me. "Huh?" I asked. "Why do you need my weight?" I stammered and stalled. There was no way I was telling that man how much I weighed.

"If you don't want to say it, just write it down on this piece of paper," he told me, obviously having dealt with the sensitive feelings of women before.

I took the sheet of paper, and after much thought, I wrote down the number that was on my driver's license, which wasn't exactly the truth. I folded the sheet over and over until it was a tiny little square, just slightly bigger than a stamp, and gave it back to the pilot.

I soon found myself in the back of the Cesna holding the U.S. Mail bag between my legs while Wayne sat up front with the pilot. Slowly, our plane began taxiing down the runway, and though our speed accelerated, we weren't going airborne. As our plane got closer and closer to the end of the airstrip with no sign of an upward slope, my heart started pounding and my thoughts started racing. The pilot had to have my correct weight to gauge the fuel. It would be my fault if we couldn't get off the ground. In fact, it looked very much like we were going to crash and burn and die!

Just as it seemed we were headed directly into the Alaska brush, from the backseat I screamed as loud as I could:

"I LIED! I LIED!"

Of course, no sooner were the words out of my mouth, than the plane launched into the air, taking us airborne, high above the trees and oblivious to my confession. The two men in front of me, however, had heard every word. My husband's smirk was evidence of that.

As soon as we arrived at our destination, I literally ran from the plane toward the lodge. While I stood catching my breath and looking up at the enormous moose antlers above the doorway, the front door burst open. Out came a native Eskimo man who stopped suddenly when he saw me. Looking me up and down, he pointed at me, and in a deep, husky voice, said: "You. Be my woman!"

My mouth went completely dry. Just then, Wayne came walking up beside me, and I grabbed his shirt. "Did you hear what he said?" I whispered to my husband, pulling him in close, and pointing to the Eskimo still standing just a few feet away.

"What?"

"He wants me to be his woman!"

Wayne paused a moment and looked at the man.

"What's he offering?"

My husband is such a kidder.

Friends, I pray that you can look at the situations in your own lives and laugh. When we can find humor in our circumstances, it's a sign that our hopes and our focus are where they need to be. Author Victor Hugo once wrote that "laughter is the sun that drives winter from the human face." I think he's right. Life is all about choices, and laughter is one choice we should all make.

I once heard a story about a man named Michael who was always in a good mood and always had something positive to say. He never saw things in a negative light, regardless of circumstances. His happy outlook drove some people crazy.

Unable to contain his curiosity, one man asked Michael how it was that he always seemed to maintain a cheerful, positive view on life. "It's easy," Michael said. "Each morning I wake up and I say to myself, 'Mike, you have two choices. You can choose to be in a good mood, or you can choose to be in a bad mood.' I choose to be in a good mood. Each time something bad happens, I can choose to be a victim or I can choose to learn from the situation. I choose to learn from it. Every time someone comes to me complaining, I can choose to accept their complaining or I can point out the positive side of life. I choose the positive side of life."

Years passed, and the man lost touch with Michael. One day, he learned that Michael had been involved in a serious accident, falling some sixty feet from a communications tower. After eighteen hours of surgery and weeks of intensive care, Michael was released from the hospital with rods in his back.

Six months after the accident, the same

man went to see Michael again. When he asked how he was doing, Michael replied, "If I were any better, I'd be twins. Wanna see my scars?"

"No thanks," the man said, "but I would like to know, what was going through your mind when you were falling?"

"The first thing that went through my mind was the well-being of my soon-to-be-born daughter," Michael replied. "Then, as I lay on the ground, I remembered that I had two choices: I could choose to live or I could choose to die. I chose to live.

"When they wheeled me into the ER and I saw the expressions on the faces of the doctors and nurses, I got really scared. In their eyes, I read 'He's a dead man.' I knew I needed to take action."

"What did you do?" the man asked.

"Well, there was a big burly nurse shouting questions at me," said Michael. "She asked if I was allergic to anything. 'Yes,' I replied. The doctors and nurses stopped working as they waited for my reply. I took a deep breath and yelled, 'Gravity!' Over their laughter, I told them, 'I am choosing to live. Operate on me as if I am alive, not dead.' "

Michael lived, thanks to the skill of the doctors, but also because of his amazing attitude. He chooses to be happy. He chooses to laugh. He chooses to make lemonade out of lemons.[9]

We can choose to either walk or run. We can choose to think negatively or act positively. We can choose to cry or we can choose to laugh, even if it sometimes means laughing through the tears. Let me encourage you to never forget that we were created for laughter. As E. E. Cummings said, "The most wasted of all days is one without laughter." The journey God has for you may end tomorrow, or it may be just beginning. Enjoy it, and look for the laughter and joy in your purpose.

■ ■ ■ ■

10
CREATED FOR
GRATITUDE

■ ■ ■ ■

Your eyes saw my unformed body.
All the days ordained for me were written
in your book
before one of them came to be.

PSALM 139:16 NIV

> As we express our gratitude, we must never forget that the highest appreciation is not to utter words, but to live by them.
> JOHN F. KENNEDY

The other morning, I was driving to my office when I noticed that an animal had been hit and was lying in the middle of the road. Roadkill. As I drove past it, trying not to look, I realized pretty quickly that this was not "normal" roadkill. My nose told me this was a dead skunk.

"Eeewwww," I said and quickly waved the air in front of me, trying to find some spot of relief, some less smelly air pocket to breathe.

It took a while for the smell to subside as I got farther down the road, and I mused over how such a potent smell could linger, despite my windows being rolled up and my inside air vents turned on. I realized I was thinking a bit negatively so I tried to find the positive. *At least I'm not the car that* hit *the skunk,* I thought with a grateful smile.

I've always been a positive person by nature, but I will tell you that I haven't always been able to feel gratitude. It's one thing to be thankful for the windfalls and unexpected blessings that come. It's quite another to be *grateful* for what we have . . . glad for the small everyday, familiar, and sometimes unremarkable yet just as meaningful graces that cross our paths. It's easy to *show* gratitude to someone; it's much harder to feel it in your heart. Yet, we were created for gratitude. We were created to be grateful to our Creator for everything He's given us. First Thessalonians 5:18 says, "Give thanks in all circumstances, for this is God's will for you in Christ Jesus" (NIV).

The psalmist recognized this in Psalm 139. His tone throughout is one of gratefulness and thankfulness. "I praise you because I am fearfully and wonderfully made. . . . How precious to me are your thoughts" (verses 14, 17 NIV).

Being created for gratitude means more than just being thankful or keeping a positive outlook on life; it means allowing our hearts to be constantly tugged toward the goodness of God. We're talking built-in radar that helps us navigate life in such a way that we're always looking for the good — and we usually find it.

When we stop long enough to think about it, we realize that the larger our gratitude bank and the more things we put in our hearts to be grateful about, the happier we feel. There's a direct correlation between being grateful and being happy.

Dennis Prager, author of *Happiness Is a Serious Problem,* describes it this way: "There is a 'secret to happiness' and it is gratitude. All happy people are grateful, and ungrateful people cannot be happy. We tend to think that it is being unhappy that leads people to complain, but it is truer to say that it is complaining that leads to people becoming unhappy. Become grateful and you will become a much happier person."[1]

Complaining only leads to more complaints. Gratitude leads to goodwill toward others and good feelings about life. It's the difference between choosing pure, fresh-tasting water or sour-tasting acidic vinegar. One restores and resuscitates; the other stings and leaves a bad taste in your mouth.

How Grateful are You?

In order to develop better patterns of gratitude, it's necessary to understand what role gratitude plays in our lives right now.

Here's a short quiz to see how you're doing in the area of gratitude.[2] After each question, choose the letter of the choice you would most likely respond with.

It's tax season and your accountant just gave you the news. You won't be getting anything back this year — instead, you owe two hundred dollars. Your response:

A. "There go our plans for a vacation this year! Now what are we supposed to do?"
B. "Well, it could have been worse, I guess."
C. "I'm happy it wasn't more, and I'm thankful that we can pay it and move on to figuring out how we're going to take that trip to the beach this summer."

Your friend calls and offers to watch the kids for you so you can run some errands. Your response:

A. "Great. Now is she going to expect me to watch her kids in return?"
B. "I wonder if I can squeeze in time for a

manicure, too. . . ."

C. "I want to think of something nice I can do for her to show how thankful I am for her friendship."

Your husband comes home from work and announces that he's getting a promotion — but it means a job transfer to another state. Your response:

A. "Absolutely not! There is no way I'm moving. I can't believe he would even think of doing this!"

B. "Well, I'm not looking forward to the moving boxes, but the pay raise will be nice."

C. "He works so hard for us, and I know he's been wanting to move up in the company for a while now. I'm going to do everything I can to support him."

If you answered mostly A's: Gratitude isn't quite your forte! Look for more ways you can bring gratitude into your life. Start a gratitude journal, or tell someone how much you appreciate her. You'll discover you like the feeling.

If you answered mostly B's: You see some things with a grateful heart, but there are definitely areas you can go even farther with. Keep working on it.

If you answered mostly C's: Gratitude is one of your special gifts. You know what it means to be thankful, and you know how much it makes you feel better when you show that gratitude to someone else.

HOPE THROUGH THE HARD TIMES

The Old Testament book of Lamentations doesn't exactly start off on an encouraging note. Okay, it doesn't even come close. Read what it says:

> How deserted lies the city, once so full of people! How like a widow is she, who once was great among the nations! She who was queen among the provinces has now become a slave. (1:1 NIV)

Lamentations is all about mourning over the destruction of Jerusalem. The prophet Jeremiah is thought to have written it, though scholars aren't completely sure. The Hebrew title of the book is *'ekah,* which, translated verbatim, means "How?"[3] Isn't that like our nature to approach bad things that happen to us with "How? How is that possible? How could that happen?"

Many of us can probably relate to this

question, though we would probably use the word *why* in place of it. Lamentations is the only book in the Bible composed solely of laments in five brief chapters. These are mournful poems usually reserved for the dead.

To lament means to wail, to cry and sob. The people who lived when Lamentations was written certainly had good reason. The Babylonians had taken over the city, and the people of Jerusalem, those who weren't killed or taken as slaves, had run to what seemed the ends of the earth. They were separated, split up, and forced out of their homes into parts unknown. Their leaders were sent into exile, and starving mothers were reduced to cannibalism (Lamentations 2:20; 4:10). Life as it was once known was no more. To say this was a sad state of affairs would be a gross understatement.

But something interesting happens when we get to Lamentations chapter 3. After pages of mourning, the author starts looking at the world through a different lens:

I remember my affliction and my wandering, the bitterness and the gall.
I well remember them, and my soul is downcast within me.

Yet this I call to mind and therefore I have
  hope:
Because of the LORD's great love we are
  not consumed, for his compassions
never fail. They are new every morning;
  great is your faithfulness.

(VERSES 19–23 NIV)

This is the high point of the book and one I want us to apply to our own lives. Despite the brokenness, despite the sheer hopelessness we sometimes find in our circumstances, we can still find hope. Because God's compassions *never* fail. Because God *is* faithful. Because He shows us that very faithfulness in a new way, in a new light, every single morning of our lives. "Because of the LORD's great love, we are not consumed." God is good. And we have a lot for which to be grateful.

AN ATTITUDE OF GRATITUDE

I ran across a book several years ago that I've read at least twice now titled *Simple Abundance: A Daybook of Comfort and Joy.* The author, Sarah Ban Breathnach, doesn't write from a Christian perspective and in fact her writing seems to border on New Age philosophy so, when reading it, I take what is true and leave the rest. What I really like are her very simple and truthful points about gratitude. When I read her suggestion about starting a gratitude journal, I thought it was a great idea.

As I've said before, every January I ask the Lord to reveal to me a word to focus on for the year. The first year I did this, I decided upon the word *gratitude*. I wanted to live my life with an attitude of gratitude, to lean toward the positive instead of allowing myself to get trapped in the mire of the negative. In an effort to remember to be grateful every day, I bought a leather-bound book and titled it "My Ode to Joy." Each morning, I wrote down five things to be happy about.

In the beginning it was difficult because I tended to overlook simple pleasures. My first lists took up whole pages as I recounted my love for my husband, children, and grandchildren. Slowly my horizons broadened, and I found joy and gratitude in things as small as the taste of a vine-ripened tomato. I came to cherish sleeping in on a Saturday morning, or sipping that first cup of coffee and watching the sun rise as I praised the Lord.

Even now, each day I write down five things I'm thankful for, and, like my goals, I usually list them by category. There's always something family-related, something personal, something about my career, and the last one is always something very simple but very profound that I'm grateful to God for that comes directly from His Word.

When I think of stories in the Bible that show gratitude, I often think about the story of the ten lepers. Do you recall it? It's found in Luke 17:11–19:

Now on his way to Jerusalem, Jesus traveled along the border between Samaria and Galilee. As he was going into a village, ten men who had leprosy met him. They stood at a distance and called out in a loud voice, "Jesus, Master, have pity on us!"

When he saw them, he said, "Go, show yourselves to the priests." And as they went, they were cleansed.

One of them, when he saw he was healed, came back, praising God in a loud voice. He threw himself at Jesus' feet and thanked him — and he was a Samaritan.

Jesus asked, "Were not all ten cleansed? Where are the other nine? Was no one found to return and give praise to God except this foreigner?" Then he said to him, "Rise and go; your faith has made you well." (NIV)

This man had an attitude of gratitude. He did not just accept the benefit of being healed. His healing went deeper — through his skin, into his heart, and down to his toes. He *ran* to Jesus to thank Him. He praised God for what had been given to him; a chance at a new life.

Notice, too, that this man was healed just like the other nine. Just like the others who left without thanking Jesus, leprosy no longer plagued his body. Yet this man chose to come back because his heart was so full. Being grateful is about being genuinely changed for the better and acknowledging it.

That last statement reminds me of what the town of Ft. Rucker, Alabama, did to show its appreciation to the boll weevil. That's right, the boll weevil. In 1915, the ugly, terrible Mexican boll weevil invaded the southeast region of the state and destroyed 60 percent of the cotton crop that farmers had worked so hard to grow. In desperation, those farmers started planting peanuts. Just two years later, the peanut industry became so profitable that Alabama farmers were harvesting more peanuts than any other state in the nation.

In gratitude, the people of the town erected a statue and inscribed these words:

"In profound appreciation of the boll weevil, and what it has done as the herald of prosperity." The instrument of their suffering had become the means of their blessing, and Alabama has the unique distinction of having the only monument in the world built in the shape of a bug.

EXPRESSING GRATITUDE TO OTHERS

After I started my gratitude journal, it wasn't long before I decided I wanted those friends I was naming in my journal to know personally how grateful I was for them. I decided to hold a Gratitude Tea so I could let them know face-to-face just how much they meant to me. I held the tea in a restaurant, but it could just as easily have been in my home.

I learned such a powerful lesson from this. I invited the people in my life who had been a blessing to me. I spent a lot of time before the day of the tea, carefully thinking through how each person had specifically blessed me. My spiritual mentor, Barb Dooley, was there. I thanked her for her godly wisdom and her example of living as a Christian wife and mother and how much I appreciated her prayers for me and my family. To my friend Lillian I spoke about how spending time with her had led to the formation of

Knitting on Gratitude

"Knitting — my Amazing Grace." — Nancie M. Wiseman, Editor, *Cast On* magazine and author of *Classic Knitted Vests* and *The Knitter's Book of Finishing Techniques*

I can think of so many things to be grateful for when it comes to knitting. Just like with my writing, I am so grateful to be able to spend time knitting wonderful blankets and sweaters and other garments that I can give away to others. I appreciate how a simple pattern can be turned into a work of art with just the right texture and color of yarn.

As knitters, we can be grateful for the friendships formed over knitting needles and yarn. I think about the joy I've felt being a part of the national board of Warm Up America. There are so many groups, big and small, all over the country who help with this rewarding organization by making 9×7 rectangles or teaching children to knit.

I am grateful for the opportunity to

> knit, to share something beautiful with others, and by doing so, experience beauty myself.

the Breakfast Club and what a blessing that had been to me. I told my cousin Cherie how special she'd been to me when we were growing up, and how much I admired her for how she took care of her younger brothers and sisters after her mother's death when she was just thirteen.

I wanted each person to know exactly how she had blessed me and why I was so honored to have her in my life. (Although many men have been a blessing to me, too, I reserved the Gratitude Tea for women.) I had each person stand when I came to her card, and I read it to her. By the end, there weren't many dry eyes in the room. But what stuck with me the most from that tea was what happened afterward. Each one came up to me and asked, "Can I keep that card?"

I decided this was a tradition I wanted to pass on to my daughters, so now we do a Gratitude Tea together, inviting the special women in our lives and taking turns sharing how each person has blessed us. Showing gratitude honors God and our friends, and it creates a lot of good feelings, which is so important in a world that's filled with so much negativity.

We all want to be appreciated; we long for it and it feels so good when we hear it. Don't wait any longer to tell the people you're grateful for why you appreciate them so much.

Over the years, I've held different teas for different groups of people in my life. I love Christmas, and although I'm a little embarrassed to admit it, I put up five Christmas trees throughout my house. That way my grandchildren know exactly which tree holds their gifts. Along with the Christmas trees there are twenty-three Nativity scenes. There's at least one in every room and sometimes more. My husband, God bless him, kindly puts up with my extravagance at Christmas. Because the house is so beautifully decorated for the holidays, I hold Christmas teas for different groups of people. One of my favorites is a tea for my swimming friends. I want them to know how much they mean to me. They're why I make it to the pool every morning, because they greet me with a smile every day, encouraging me and helping me exercise. Many of them have been swimming for

years and are in their seventies and eighties.
They inspire me and keep me motivated.

BE GRATEFUL IN EVERYTHING

Gratitude doesn't just concern family and
friends. Over the years, I've tried to employ
gratitude in my professional life as well.
There are a number of wonderful profes-
sionals who have assisted me in my career.
About ten years ago, I looked for a way to
thank local booksellers for their ongoing
support of me and my books. That Valen-
tine's Day lunch has now become a tradition. Each February I take the local booksellers and librarians to lunch. Naturally, we
talk about books, which they love as much
as I do. Over the years, I've gained valuable
insights and remarkable bits of wisdom
from these booklovers. Because of the
luncheons, they've gotten to know one
another and have also become good friends.

I searched for an idea that would let my
readers know that I appreciated their faithful support of me and my books. After
brainstorming, I came up with the idea of
putting together a little family recipe book
and mailing it out in time for Christmas. It
was my way of saying thanks for their
encouragement and support. Through that,
I became a value-added author to my read-

ers, someone who doesn't just deliver books, but seeks to keep that genuine connection and relationship with anyone who picks up one of my books. Tradition continues today with yearly newsletters, bookmarks, and calendar stickers and in response, I have very loyal readers who feel a personal connection to me, and me to them. They tell me what they like and don't like, and their feedback has helped shape my career.

PASSING ON THE GIFT OF GRATITUDE

One of the bonuses of working on bringing more gratitude into your life is that it rubs off on your children, too. I see it in the way my children live their lives. One example is Jody, my oldest, who manages the Victorian Rose Tea Room and Springhouse Dolls and Gifts, the two businesses my husband and I own. She has an attitude of gratitude with the employees and with the customers.

Karol Ladd is the author of *The Power of a Positive Mom,* and she makes the good point that attitudes are contagious. One of her tips for encouraging gratitude in children is to use dinnertime to talk about what the family can be thankful for. Bedtime is also another easy opportunity to thank God with your children for all of the wonderful things that happened during the day.

Ladd suggests helping children create what she calls a "Grateful Poster." The poster can be decorated with markers, glitter, stickers — anything that your children want to add to make it theirs. Then, each day, take time with your child to write a one-sentence statement that thanks God for His blessings, large and small. This will help your children focus on thankful thoughts and hopefully develop a regular habit of gratitude that will continue into their adult lives.[4]

THE ART OF BEING CONTENT

I heard a story recently about a lady who always seemed to complain about everything and everybody. Finally, her minister found something she couldn't complain about. The lady's crop of potatoes was the finest for miles around. He said to her, "For once you must be pleased. Everyone is saying how splendid your potatoes are this year."

The lady glared at him and said, "They aren't so bad, *but where are the rotten ones for the pigs?*"

Instead of being grateful, she was grouchy. Instead of realizing her great blessing, she took it for granted. It was as though she was saying, "So what? I always have good potatoes, but there should be more."[5]

Here is where the rubber meets the road. To learn to be grateful, we must learn to be content. How content do you feel today? Are you grateful for what you have, or are you always looking ahead to what tomorrow may bring? Are you content with the small things, or are the big, seemingly unreachable things eating you up inside and destroying what happiness you might have?

Stop for a moment, put this book down, and look at yourself in the mirror. What is the first glimpse of your face like? Do your eyes look bright? Or are they red and run down? Is your mouth in a natural, pleasant spot, or are the corners drooping a bit? Is there a light in your eyes, or do they look dull and lacking life? Do you look haggard or upbeat? Can you honestly see happiness when you look at yourself, or do you see pent-up longing and wishes for what others already have?

Friends, I can't stress enough that no amount of success in the world, no amount of intensity to accomplish our dreams, is going to matter if we can't come to a place where we are content with what we have. Now, I'm not saying you should give up your dreams; hardly — I wouldn't have a reason to write this book if I were saying that! I am saying that in the midst of pursuing success and dreams and purpose, we must remember to be content no matter what circumstances we find ourselves in, as we work toward achieving our goals.

As Paul says in Philippians 4:12:

> I know what it is to be in need, and I know what it is to have plenty.
> I have learned the secret of being content in any and every situation,
> whether well fed or hungry, whether living in plenty or in want. (NIV)

Isn't that powerful? What would it be like if we could always be content in every situation? Wouldn't we be happier? Wouldn't we feel more alive? I imagine it would be like lifting a great weight off our shoulders, the same sense of freedom that many of us experienced when we gave our hearts to Christ.

Hebrews 13:5 says, "Keep your lives free from the love of money and be content with what you have, because God has said, 'Never will I leave you; never will I forsake you' " (NIV).

In his book *Jesus, Lord of Your Personality,*

pastor Bob Russell points out that having a lot doesn't tend to produce a grateful spirit:

Have you had a taste of the best this world has to offer? You went to Hawaii once on vacation, so now it's harder for you to enjoy the state park. You've eaten a steak at Morton's, so it's harder to be thankful for a meal at Ponderosa. You've driven a Jaguar, so now you can't be as content with your used Chevrolet. You've cheered for a national champion, so now it's difficult to be grateful when your team has a good season but doesn't take home the title. . . .

Generally speaking, the more we have, the less grateful we are. It should be the opposite; the more we have, the more thankful we should be. But it usually doesn't work that way, does it?

It is a rare person who, when his cup frequently runs over, can give thanks to God instead of complaining about the limited size of his mug![6]

Think about what it must have been like for the Israelites after they left Egypt. God had promised them a land of milk and honey, or, in more contemporary terms, steak and lobster. After so many years of slavery and hard times, they were ready! But what happened? After just a few days in the desert, folks were ready to go back to Egypt — the very place where they were oppressed as slaves! They were hot, they were tired, and they were hungry. To paraphrase, they told Moses and Aaron that they might as well go back where they were under Pharaoh's rule, because at least then they weren't starving (Exodus 16:3).

They were grumbling! They were complaining! Instead of seeing the situation for the good, that they were on their way to bigger and better things than they'd had, they could see only their present circumstances, which looked so bad in their eyes, they remembered their past as being a whole lot better than it actually was.

God in all His compassion heard their complaints and met the Israelites' need by providing manna from the sky in the mornings, "bread from heaven" the Bible calls it, and quail meat in the evenings. But He had one request: that they take only what they needed each day. No storing. No hoarding.

Unfortunately, there will always be people who don't listen to God. The ones who ignored what Moses told them learned very quickly why it's important to listen when they discovered that the food they had squirreled away back in their tents became infested with maggots and moldy bacteria that made it stink when they went to retrieve it the next day.

You see, God wanted them to take only what they needed each day. Everyone had exactly what they needed, each and every day. The only time this changed was the night before the Sabbath, when God provided a double portion so the people would not have to work the following day. God was trying to teach them to depend on Him. And there is the lesson we need to learn ourselves.

You see, the Israelites didn't know how to be content. They kept thinking, *Well, what about tomorrow? What if help doesn't come after today? What then?* And yet the art of contentment is having the ability to be happy with today. The Israelites struggled with being grateful. And they received a forty-year lesson because of it.

Do you ever feel like the Israelites? So worried about tomorrow that you can't enjoy today? I know I've had days like that. I've had weeks and months like that! Just as Satan wants to take away our joy and laughter, he wants to also rob us of our contentment. Because when we're experiencing discontent or misery, we're distracted from our purpose and our focus. Don't let him win.

Instead, learn how to connect gratitude and contentment into the pattern God's designed for you. Here are some suggestions:

Be Intentional in Your Gratitude

Just like with our relationships and our work and with balance, we must look for ways to practice gratitude. Whether it's writing something down in a journal, making it a habit to write thank-you notes, or just simply saying out loud, "I am grateful for . . ." In the morning when we get in the car, we can look for ways to remind ourselves of what we're grateful for.

Be Smart in Your Spending

Be thankful for what you have, but understand that you don't have to have it all! Buying stuff only gets us more stuff — and in the end, we can't take it with us. Live below your means.

Enjoy Your Day *Today*

Stop looking to tomorrow with "I wishes" and "If only's." Find contentment for what life has brought you today. It's okay to look ahead, to plan and to dream. We cross a line, though, when plans and dreams keep us always looking into the future and cause us to miss our *now*.

Learn How to Enjoy the Simple Things

When you're stuck in traffic, put in an audiobook and give God a prayer of thanks for the little bit of extra time you have to listen to something good. Be happy with the blue sky and the sunshine, or the rain coming down that will water your grass so you don't have to. Appreciate every picture your kindergartner brings home because you realize he won't be little forever.

Find Ways to Bring "A Smile a Day"

Let this be your daily game: to put a smile on someone else's face. It could be complimenting a store clerk on her fast service, or maybe calling a friend who needs a pick-me-up. Whatever it is, look for ways to put a smile on someone else's face. When you do, chances are you'll also find a smile on yours.

Once we learn to accept God's provision and be content with what we are given, we can truly find the good in whatever circumstances God brings to us. That attitude of gratitude pushes selfish thoughts out, helping us continue to focus on our purpose and making it all the easier to be what we will discuss in the next chapter: a blessing to others.

■ ■ ■ ■

11
CREATED FOR BLESSING

■ ■ ■ ■

How precious to me are your thoughts, O
  God!
How vast is the sum of them!

PSALM 139:17 NIV

May God give you . . . For every storm a rainbow, for every tear a smile, for every care a promise and a blessing in each trial. For every problem life sends, a faithful friend to share, for every sigh a sweet song and an answer for each prayer.

IRISH BLESSING

We are a people who enjoy blessings. Think about it. We bless each other when we sneeze and we bless each other's hearts when something goes wrong. We "say the blessing" when we sit down to eat, and we bless the cook before we say amen. We are never *lucky* — only blessed.

As God's faithful, we're constantly on the lookout for His blessings. We hold on to verses like Psalm 5:12, which says, "O LORD, you bless the righteous; you surround them with your favor" (NIV); or Psalm 37:22, which reads, "Those the LORD blesses will inherit the land" (NIV). The #1 nonfiction bestseller for 2001, selling more than 8 million copies, was the *Prayer of Jabez:* "Oh, that you would bless me and enlarge my territory! Let your hand be with me, and keep me from harm so that I will be free from pain" (1 Chronicles 4:10 NIV). This is important when we're thinking about our purpose because if there is anything we especially want, it's to have God's blessings on our purpose!

When we receive a blessing, we receive God's divine, unmerited favor. We find God's favor mentioned throughout the Bible; we see His favor with Noah (Genesis 6:8), with Moses, Gideon, David, and Mary, to name a few. We see God's favor in our own lives when we find our prayers answered or God sends unexpected surprises that brighten our days.

When I think of God's blessings, I think of His grace. God doesn't have to bless us, but He does it anyway. His is an unconditional love that I don't think any of us will fully understand until we see Him face-to-face. As John writes in the Bible, "From the fullness of his grace we have all received one blessing after another" (John 1:16 NIV).

It is because of God's grace that we receive His blessings.

There's no amount of goal-setting, success strategy, or just plain hard work you can do to earn God's grace. And yet, it's so easy for us to fall into working to please God, instead of accepting His love and the free blessings He has for us.

That reminds me of the story Charles Stanley tells about a professor he once had who wanted to teach his students about grace. At the end of his course on evangelism, he passed out the final exam to his students, cautioning them to be sure to read it all the way through before they tried to answer any of the questions. The same warning was written on the front page of the test itself. As the students began to read the questions, it became very clear that the preparation each had taken for the exam wasn't nearly enough.

The questions got harder and harder and some of the test-takers groaned out loud. It was an impossible exam — that is, until the students got to the last page — where they discovered a note from the professor. It read: "You have a choice. You can either complete the exam as given or sign your name at the bottom and, in doing so, receive an A for this assignment."

The classroom got quiet as the stunned students thought about the choice. "Was he serious? Just sign it and get an A?" Slowly, they got the point, and one by one each student got up, turned in the test, and silently left the room.

Afterward Stanley talked with the professor about the test, and his teacher shared some of the reactions he had received through the years.

Some students began taking the exam without reading it all the way through, and they sweated it out for the entire two hours of class time before reaching the last page.

Others read the first couple of pages, became angry, turned the test in blank, and stormed out of the room without signing it. They never realized what was available, and as a result, they lost out totally.

One fellow, however, read the entire test, including the note at the end, but decided to take the exam anyway. He did not want any gifts; he wanted to earn his grade. And he did. He made a C+, but he could easily have had an A.[1]

How many of us could easily scribble our name and leave willy-nilly? It would be hard, wouldn't it? Would you be suspicious, thinking there was some trick to it? Or would you be extremely grateful, accepting the grace extended to you with thanks and appreciation?

How many of us are like that last guy? Even when God puts His blessings right in front of us for the taking, we turn inward, stubbornly stepping over the blessing, determined to earn it ourselves. After all, what's your first response when someone does something nice for you? *I need to return the favor. . . .* What's your reaction when someone unexpectedly brings you a gift? *Oh, I don't have a gift for her. . . . Now I have to go buy something.* But God's gifts are given with grace; no hidden strings, no extra-duty list we have to check off. God's grace is free. God's blessings are free. We just have to accept them.

There's not a lot in life that's free. Unfortunately, the media have conditioned us to be cynical about anything that's said to be free. Car salesmen offer "free" warranties, only to reveal later that the price of the warranty was rolled into the sticker price of the car. TV and radio commercials scream, "Free! Free!" but a quick check of the fine print says it's not necessarily so. But God's grace is free. It's revealed through His incredible, overwhelming love for each of us. He doesn't give it with the expectation of something in return. He doesn't give it with a weight hanging over our heads ready to crush us the moment we mess up. He gives it freely. And readily. With much, much love. We must only be ready to receive. And to love back.

THE BLESSING OF GRACE

One of my favorite writers is Philip Yancey, author of *What's So Amazing about Grace?* Philip was actually on my list of thirty people I'd like to meet, and I had the honor of meeting him over dinner one year while in Denver. I was struck by his practical faith and his intelligence. He's written some of the most profound books on our faith that I've ever read.

In *What's So Amazing about Grace?*, Philip writes:

Grace means there is nothing we can do to make God love us more — no amount of spiritual calisthenics and renunciations, no amount of knowledge gained from seminaries, no amount of crusading on behalf of righteous causes. And grace means there is nothing we can do to make God love us less. . . . Grace means that God already loves us as much an infinite God can possibly love.[2]

336

Grace in itself is a blessing that God bestows on us. It isn't a result of being measured and found deserving; it's the good things that God wants to provide simply because He loves us and He wishes the best for us.

We were created for blessing. I talked earlier in the book about how hard it is sometimes as Christians to think about wanting success. There is nothing wrong with wanting God's blessings or His grace. The fine line we must walk, however, is when we expect those blessings yet we are unwilling or unaware of the opportunities we have to be a blessing to others.

CREATED TO BLESS OTHERS

I'm profoundly grateful for all of the blessings God has poured into my life. I'm grateful for the hard times, too, because they make me appreciate the blessings even more. And while it's only natural that we desire good things, blessings, to fill our lives, I believe we have to be aware of the dangers we can encounter, the traps we can fall into, when we become so focused on *receiving* the blessings that we forget about *giving* the blessings. I often share with the writers in my writing workshops that it's important to seek out mentors, but it's just as important to be a mentor to someone else. It's important to give as much as we receive. I could argue that we should strive to give even more than what we get back. What I've discovered is that, quite often, the more you give, the more you receive in return.

The day I ran across what God tells Abraham in Genesis 12:2 was a day that changed my life for the better: "I will make you into a great nation and I will bless you; I will make your name great, and *you will be a blessing*" (NIV, emphasis mine).

Those words practically highlighted themselves in my Bible. That was my mission statement; that's what I knew God was instructing me to do with my life. I think about that verse a lot and I apply it — to the books I write and the stories I tell. I constantly ask myself, how will this bless someone else?

I think about the year that both of my boys were in college. They were struggling with what to buy their grandparents for Christmas, since both of them were short on money. They wanted my mom and dad to know how much they loved them, but finding a gift within their price range became more and more of a challenge as they got older and out on their own.

Then one Thanksgiving, close to the end

of my father's life, he casually mentioned how much he used to love decorating the house with lights every Christmas. He couldn't any longer, and that saddened him.

Shortly after that conversation with their grandpa, Ted and Dale came to me with an idea. They wanted to drive to Yakima (a good three hours from our home) and decorate the outside of their grandparents' home for Christmas. Then in January, they'd drive back and take everything down. This would be their Christmas gift to their grandparents.

The boys did a stellar job of it. I pitched in and purchased the necessary supplies, and the boys spent two days stringing lights all around the outside of the house. Every bush, plant, and tree trunk in sight was wrapped in lights. My dad beamed with pride that his house was the most brilliantly lit home in the neighborhood. This time with my parents was the best gift my two sons could ever have given them.

Ted and Dale had such a good time with their grandparents, and each other, that they returned every couple of months and completed necessary tasks around the house that my father could no longer do. It meant the world to my parents, who treasured this special gift more than anything the boys could have purchased.

I learned a valuable lesson from my sons that year. An extra toy under the tree for the grandchildren wouldn't mean half as much as playing a game of Monopoly with them, or holding a special tea party complete with fancy hats and clothes. The gift of time is a blessing that no monetary gift can ever replace.

Finding ways to give blessings to others requires time, a willingness to be intentional, and a willingness to love. Over the years, God has taught me what have been at times shocking lessons about the power of love. Probably the most dynamic story is about my friendship with Willie Jackson and Darryl Pruitt, two prisoners I became acquainted with through a prison ministry with my church. It was through them that I met Philip Yancey and talked to Chuck Colson from Prison Fellowship. I started Bible study lessons with both men, I prayed for them, and my family befriended them. We wrote to Willie for seven years and rejoiced when he was paroled. Unfortunately, we only heard from him twice after that. We continue to pray for him and place him in God's hands. Darryl remains incarcerated.

Through a Prison Fellowship contact, I met Andre Supek, who claimed he wanted nothing to do with God or religion. I ignored that statement and asked him if he had any questions about the Lord. He wrote back: "Mrs. Macomber, you're obviously a nice lady, and I guess finding religion for others is all good and well, but all this God stuff just isn't for me."

I wasn't giving up that easily. I told Andre that God had an incredible offer for him. He wanted to exchange Andre's chains for a pair of wings. Andre politely refused. Each morning I prayed, day after day, week after week. Andre wrote occasionally, and I, as time allowed, answered, each time reminding him of God's offer.

Then, on April 19, 1997, Andre gave his life to Christ. He wrote that it had been so long since he'd cried that the tears felt like acid on his cheeks.

When I was asked to join the prison ministry at my church I went into it kicking and fighting, embarrassed to be writing men and women in prison. I had a different image of myself, and writing letters to prisoners certainly didn't fit with how I thought I should be using my skills. Yet, I have no doubt that the Lord asked me to do this.

Several years ago, when I first started writing to these men to tell them about Jesus, I started praying for them. I'd never known anyone in prison and wasn't sure how to pray. The Lord put Ephesians 3:17–18 on my heart: "I pray that you, being rooted and established in love, may have power, together with all the saints, to grasp how wide and long and high and deep is the love of Christ" (NIV). This was my prayer for Willie, Darryl, and Andre, but it was I who experienced the love of God, I who was blessed, I who received.

During the last ten years of working with the prison ministry, the Lord blessed my spiritual life unlike any other time I can remember. My faith was rejuvenated, and God allowed me to see incredible results.

THE BLESSING OF PRAYER

Much of what happened with Andre and the others had to do with prayer, and that brings up an important point. We can bless others when we pray for them.

Prayer can be a powerful weapon; a powerful way to help those we care about. The Bible says that we have only to pray and we will receive (Matthew 21:22; Mark 11:24); our prayers are "powerful and effective" (James 5:16 NIV).

Four years ago, I started choosing three people each year to devote special prayer to.

They don't know I'm praying for them on a daily basis. At some point in the year I purchase a Bible to give them and thank them for being in my life. I ask the Holy Spirit to give them a spiritual hunger to know Christ and to discover His love for them in a profound and personal way.

One of the first I ever prayed for was Susan Plunkett, another writer who had moved to Seattle from Texas. I didn't think it was coincidence that God moved her just down the block from me. I didn't know her very well, but she was good friends with another writer who lived in the area. Susan and I went to lunch on the day of the big Seattle earthquake in 2001. As I talked with her, I sensed in Susan a spiritual hunger. I felt she was ready to know God.

I started praying in earnest for Susan, claiming her for the Lord, and as I did, my heart went out to her. That's what happens when we pray for people; when we lift someone to Jesus, He keeps that person front and center in our life. That's why I say, if we're mad or don't get along with someone, the best way to fix that relationship is to pray for that person. It's hard to get started, but once we do, it's amazing what God can do with that relationship we thought was doomed to fail.

So I prayed for Susan, invited her to a Bible study, and even bought her the resources she needed to get started and attended the study with her.

I have to tell you, the day she came to the Lord was like an explosion! Susan was soon on fire for the Lord. The next thing I knew, her sister, her brother-in-law, and her sister's family had all either asked Christ into their lives for the first time or renewed their faith in Christ. It happened as quick as wildfire. When the time came for her to be baptized, Susan asked me to be the one to baptize her. It was one of the greatest honors of my life to stand with my friend as she made her commitment known publicly.

Not every person I've prayed for has stepped forward to commit to Christ. One friend has repeatedly declined; choosing, instead, to follow a New Age philosophy. But I continue to lift her before the Lord, and trust that in His time, and in His own way, He will reveal Himself to Theresa. There have been a number of situations where God has asked me to plant seeds of blessing, blessings that I may never see with my own eyes but that I must trust will bear fruit in God's timing.

It seemed to me that just about the time my parenting skills were down pat, I had an

Knitting on Blessing

When I think about blessings, I often think about my knitting. One of the joys of knitting is giving to others. What am I going to do with a hundred sweaters? I certainly don't want to make them all for myself — I want to give them away to the people I love.

I barely remember my grandmother; she died when I was only four or five years old. But I was told that she was a consummate crocheter. My older cousins remember that she could crochet with her eyes closed — she would actually sleep in her rocking chair and her hands would keep crocheting away. Since no one in my immediate family knitted, I'm sure I must have gotten my love for yarn and wool from my grandmother.

When I was twelve, my mother took me to the yarn store, bought me yarn and needles, and left me at the store for the afternoon so I could learn how to knit. I came home and made my mother a beautiful purple vest. She still had that purple vest when she died in

> March 2005. Knitting is certainly a way
> of expressing love, of giving blessings
> to other people. It's been around for
> thousands of years. In fact, knitted
> items have been found in the tombs of
> pharaohs.

empty nest. So I decided to become a mentor. I loved the idea, contacted the local high school, and asked to work with a girl who was interested in becoming a writer. In my mind's eye, I pictured God sending me someone like myself, eager to learn everything there is to know about writing. As a teenager I would have given just about anything to meet a real writer. Instead, God sent me Syrena. An eighteen-year-old single welfare mother, who worked weekends at a topless bar and was a practicing witch. (For those of you who've read the Blossom Street books, Alix is modeled after Syrena.)

The last thing Syrena wanted to hear about was God. "Been there, done that, not interested." But God has given me a genuine love for her, and when His love is backed by His power, that makes all the difference in the world. I met with Syrena for a number of years and even hired her to be part of my office staff for a time. She's drifted in and out of my life. I've claimed Syrena for Christ, and I believe one day she will know Him as her Lord and Savior. She knows she can come to me whenever she needs help or prayer and that I'll be there for her.

Passing along blessings can quickly create a chain reaction. This last summer, I was able to get involved with Northwest Family Life, a Christian organization that helps people in the inner city. They had a fire that destroyed their building and were trying to decide how to best spend the insurance money. The director had been reading my Blossom Street series of books and so she decided to open a yarn store in an area that is populated by a widely diverse international community. With the insurance money and some seed money, they built a beautiful yarn store that is now frequented by women in the area coming in off the streets wanting to learn how to knit. Judges are even sending prostitutes to the store to learn how to knit for community service. Mothers who live in poor neighborhoods are learning how to create beautiful blankets and clothes. Without the word *church* on their door, this store is opening doors to God with the people that they're ministering to.

So much of what we can do to bless others doesn't have to have money attached. Maybe that's what keeps so many people from helping someone else — we have a fear that we'll be committed for the long haul, or it will cost us more than we're willing to pay. But how much commitment does it take to walk up to a soldier in uniform in an airport, shake his hand, and thank him for the service he's doing for our country? How much does it cost us to smile at the clerk in the checkout line and thank her for helping us? How much effort does it take to help an older neighbor by returning her trash can from the curb? Not much, but the goodwill and the blessing we create from those small acts of kindness are priceless.

The Random Acts of Kindness Foundation, based in Denver, Colorado, is an organization that encourages people "to practice kindness and to 'pass it on' to others." They report that studies show that being kind to others helps improve your health, both physical and mental. Some of these benefits include:

- A diminished effect of diseases and disorders, serious and minor, psychological and physical.

- The improvement of stress-related health problems after performing kind acts. Helping other people reverses feelings of depression, supplies social contact, and decreases feelings of hostility and isolation that can cause stress, overeating, ulcers, etc. A drop in stress may, for some people, decrease the constriction within the lungs that leads to asthma attacks.
- Enhanced feelings of joy, emotional resilience, and vigor. It can also reduce an unhealthy sense of isolation.
- A decrease in both the intensity and the awareness of physical pain.
- An increased sense of self-worth, greater happiness, and optimism, as well as a decrease in feelings of helplessness and depression.[3]

Mike Brown lives in Sandpoint, Idaho, and is the owner of a manufactured-home retail business. In the frigid winter of 2004, he learned that William and Clara DeMers had watched their house burn to the ground, leaving the couple homeless. He thought about an older sixty-five-foot, single-wide trailer he had just received as a trade-in, something he would normally have turned around and sold. Instead, he decided to give it to the DeMerses.

"I didn't think twice about it," Brown said. "This community has always been good to me, and I wanted to give something back. I had a good year and felt blessed.

"Besides, these people needed shelter. It seemed like the right thing to do."

Two years later, the businessman saw his act of kindness turn into a boomerang of blessings. The DeMerses showed up in his office one day after selling a five-acre piece of property and purchased the largest and most expensive double-wide trailer home his company had available. Even better, the couple donated the home that Brown had given them to another family in need.[4]

When we pass a blessing on to someone, not only do we impact that person, but we raise the potential for even more blessings to be passed on. It's like the commercial Liberty Mutual created that features various people, all strangers, passing little acts of kindness forward, taking responsibility for helping others. A man stops and picks up the doll that a little girl has dropped. Her mother then prevents a man's coffee cup from toppling over. Another man helps someone up who has fallen. Little acts of kindness that keep going, as they're passed from one person to another. . . .

Steve Elliott wrote a book in 2005 called *The Grassfire Effect: How One Small Spark Can Change Your World.* It focuses on the notion that all it takes is a simple idea, "a spark of creativity, to spread a grassfire of healthy change as well as personal and business success." I believe it's the same with blessing. All it takes is one person being willing to make a difference in someone else's day, someone else's life, for a grassfire of blessing to spread through an office, through a church, through a community, through our world.

Be the spark that starts that fire of blessing today, and watch how God blesses you in return.

■ ■ ■ ■

12
CREATED FOR WORSHIP

■ ■ ■ ■

Were I to count them,
they would outnumber the grains of sand.
When I awake, I am still with you.
                    PSALM 139:18 NIV

We are called to an everlasting
preoccupation with God.

A. W. TOZER

This is the final chapter of our journey
together and what I consider to be the
anchor of everything we've talked about up
to this point. I saved the best for last. Let's
discuss worship — the time we spend talking with and listening to our Creator, our
Lord, our Comforter, and our Hope. The
entire chapter of Psalm 139 creates imagery
and a feeling of worship. In fact, the book
of Psalms is one book of the Bible I often
use as a part of my worship time. Often, I'll
open to Psalms and look through verses,
underlining those that stand out.

No amount of work, no amount of risk,
passion, understanding my purpose, or
achieving balance in the pursuit of success

— none of that holds a candle to the greatest thing that's impacted my life, and that's spending time in consistent worship and prayer. This has been ongoing since I made a commitment to Jesus Christ all those years ago. I doubt I would have found my purpose without that lifeline to my Creator. Without being grounded in worship, I would've walked the tightrope of risk-taking without any net and risked the possibility of falling off before achieving my dreams.

Worship has many definitions, depending on who you ask. Some people think of worship as the time of singing before the sermon at church, or the entire service may be considered a worship time. Some like to spend their time in worship on the golf course; after all, God made those beautiful trees and blue sky, didn't He? I've even known people who spend their Sunday mornings in an art museum gazing at beautiful paintings and sculpture. Their rationale is God is beauty, so that's worship, right?

A lot of people think worship is describing the music a particular church offers. If you've been the member of a church at any point in the last twenty years, you have no doubt experienced "worship wars" to some degree. Again, I think we miss the true heart of worship when we get caught up in a debate about whether singing to an organ and piano or to a rock band makes us more holy.

What Is Worship?

So what exactly is worship? Is it the things I've listed above, or is it something more? A while back, I ran across a wonderful series about this very subject by Rev. Dr. Mark D. Roberts, the senior pastor of Irvine Presbyterian Church in Irvine, California. Before joining the congregation there, he served on the staff of First Presbyterian Church of Hollywood.

In "The Soul of Worship," Roberts writes that "whatever else we might believe about Christian worship, *it is essentially and necessarily a response to God.* It is our reaction to a God who has initiated relationship with us, reaching out to us in love and grace through Jesus Christ"[1] (emphasis in original).

God wants us to worship Him. He longs for that relationship with us. And ultimately, we long for that relationship as well, although sometimes we don't realize it. There is a deep part of us that desires worship because we were created to desire it. Sometimes we unintentionally shove it down and ignore it, but it is still there. We are happiest doing what God created us to do.

The word *worship* comes from an old English word that contains the ideas of honor and worth. When we worship God, we recognize who He is, and what He does; we honor Him.[2]

Most people think of worship as formal; they go to church, sit in a pew, and go home afterward to a big dinner. Worship isn't just singing in the choir or passing Communion; it's not something that's supposed to be compartmentalized or divided up; it should be part of our everyday lives. For me, worship starts first thing in the morning when I take that hour and a half to pray and study and reflect on what God's doing in my life.

It's not just about my talking to Him; it is equally important for me to listen to what He's telling me, letting me know, "This is your day; let's plan it; let's think about it."

Worshipping Christ is very much an intimate part of my daily life. It's both an action and an attitude, one of reverence and respect. That morning time I spend is worship, from the devotionals I read to the writing I do in my journals, conveying my thoughts to God. It's the simple things. God not only wants me to be His child Monday morning, He wants me to remember Him Tuesday afternoon and the whole week through. He wants me to live my life through a lens of His choosing, one that takes what I learn through intimate worship and applies it on a day-to-day basis. A Christian worldview.

Charles Colson writes in his now-classic *How Now Shall We Live?* that "genuine Christianity is more than a relationship with Jesus . . . church attendance, Bible study, and works of charity. It is more than discipleship, more than believing a system of doctrines about God. Genuine Christianity is a way of seeing and comprehending all reality. It is a worldview."[3]

Whether someone has a personal relationship with Christ or not, everyone has a worldview. It is the core of beliefs that make you who you are. I believe that, as Christians, worship can be the core of what directs our worldview. When we have that intimate time with God, we have a constant, consistent thinking and understanding of the things that are important to our heavenly Father.

There are certain actions we repeat so often that we don't really have to think about them before we do them. Riding a bike, swimming in the pool, or getting dressed in the morning makes use of what doctors and scientists call muscle memory — the brain and the muscle learn together, and, as a result, when the necessary action is required, the response is automatic.

Friends, a Christian worldview requires spiritual muscle memory, an automatic but natural response of the heart and life, living out God's love on a day-to-day basis. There is no greater way to develop that memory than through the act of worship.

THE CORPORATE PART OF WORSHIP

A pastor went to see a man who attended church infrequently. The man was sitting before a fire, watching the warm glow of the coals. It was a cold winter day, but the coals were red hot and the fire was warm. The pastor urged the man to be more faithful in meeting with the people of God, but the man didn't seem to be getting the message.

"I think I can worship as well alone as at church," he told the preacher.

After reflecting for a moment, the pastor took the tongs beside the fireplace, lifted a live coal from the fire, and set it down at the side of the grate. As they watched, its color turned to gray and the heat slowly died. The church member got the point.

After a long pause, he said, "I'll be in

church on Sunday."[4]

I love this story because it illustrates so beautifully the importance of worshipping together in a corporate setting. Whether that takes the form of a traditional congregation or a more contemporary venue such as a house church, God designed us to need one another, to worship Him together. Look at how the early church did it:

> All the believers were together and had everything in common. Selling their possessions and goods, they gave to anyone as he had need. Every day they continued to meet together in the temple courts. They broke bread in their homes and ate together with glad and sincere hearts, praising God and enjoying the favor of all the people. And the Lord added to their number daily those who were being saved. (ACTS 2:44–47 NIV)

This church did life together! They shared their ups and downs, trials and joys, and everything in between.

In 2005, the Gallup poll did an interesting study, commissioned by Group Publishing, Inc., on how friendship affects faith. They found strong evidence that members of a congregation were able to live out their faith in an atmosphere that welcomed and fostered friendships more fully than in isolation. A person's spiritual commitment actually appeared to be greater when that person's best friend was in the same church — more than 82 percent of those with best friends "strongly agreed" that they were spiritually committed individuals; 74 percent "strongly agreed" that their faith was involved in every aspect of their lives; and 69 percent spent time in worship or prayer every day.[5]

It doesn't take an official poll to know that we thrive better when we're with other people. But there's a growing danger that threatens this important group component. Busyness. We have only to look at the church attendance scale to see that Sunday mornings for most churches typically get the largest portion of attendance, with Sunday nights and Wednesday nights coming in at a much lower number and not always in that order. As much as we need other people, most families are overwhelmed with not having enough time for each other, let alone for additional activities and friendships. Instead of our homes being places of fellowship, they have become hiding places where we frown if someone knocks at the door, or fret if a friend invites herself over for a chat.

Busyness can truly dampen our efforts to worship. Christian author and speaker Jill Briscoe wrote, "We can worry or we can worship. Strangely enough, busy people find it a whole lot easier to worry than to worship."[6] And yet, when we allow ourselves to take time to worship, and *worship together,* our worries decrease exponentially.

THE INTIMACY OF INDIVIDUAL WORSHIP

As important as corporate worship is, intimate individual worship is equally needed in our lives. Sometimes I think we use church to replace individual worship and with it our responsibility to the personal relationship we have with God. We need to take care to balance both.

Let's go back to that word: *responsibility.* Did you know we are responsible for initiating worship? That we are actually commanded to worship? Look at what God's Word says:

One of the teachers of the law came and heard them debating. Noticing that Jesus had given them a good answer, he asked him, "Of all the commandments, which is the most important?"

"The most important one," answered

Jesus, "is this: 'Hear, O Israel, the Lord our God, the Lord is one. Love the Lord your God with all your heart and with all your soul and with all your mind and with all your strength.'" (MARK 12:28–30 NIV)

We are commanded to love God with our hearts. Our souls. Our minds. Our strength. With every part of who and what we are. We do that through worship. Notice that Jesus calls this commandment "the most important one." Unfortunately, I think that sometimes we forget the Greatest Commandment and replace it instead with the Great Commission, which we find in Matthew 28:19–20:

Therefore go and make disciples of all nations, baptizing them in the name of the Father and of the Son and of the Holy Spirit, and teaching them to obey everything I have commanded you. And surely I am with you always, to the very end of the age. (NIV)

How can we share His love and His teachings with the nations if we do not first have those things in our own hearts? This is why intimate worship is so important and so necessary if we want to see our relationship with God grow.

The Barna Group did a nationwide survey back in 2005 that examined the spiritual development of Christians. When it came to maintaining healthy relationships, serving other people, living out their faith, leading their families spiritually, and worshipping God, most people rated themselves as quite average, with less-than-average ratings for knowing the Bible and sharing their faith with others.

I find it striking that the majority of adults who were polled in this survey considered themselves to be average in each of the spiritual dimensions they were asked about.

God does not want us to be average; not in our work, not in our dreams, and certainly not in our worship. Let me challenge you today as you begin to work on all the different things we've talked about throughout the book, to place worship front and center and above everything else. Be above average; be completely passionate for God!

TALKING WITH GOD

One of the ways we can increase our passion, our excitement for worship, is by spending more time in prayer — conversation with God.

I grew up around a very formal form of

prayer, and after I made my commitment to Christ, I remember hearing my pastor give a sermon on the topic of prayer. He said that prayer was like talking to your father. This isn't a new concept to many, but at the time, it was to me. My dad owned an upholstery shop, so it was very natural for me to imagine, the next time I prayed, talking to Jesus in an upholstery shop, which looked very much like a carpenter's workshop. As I was praying and talking to Jesus, sharing with Him my concerns, I pictured Jesus turning and looking at me and saying, "Debbie, I have such wonderful books for you to write in heaven." Not only was my perspective on prayer changed, but also my whole perspective on the afterlife. God has work for us to do in heaven as well. The things that bring us joy on earth will be multiplied in heaven.

Becky Tirabassi is the author of *Let Prayer Change Your Life*. She shares her own experience with prayer and the day she made a commitment to God to pray for one hour every day. She writes out her prayers, as I do, and she recommends this as a way to transcribe our conversations with God.

I mention Becky not because she prays for an hour a day, but because she prays every day. Discipline is required with our

Knitting on Prayer

I often bring prayer into my knitting. Especially when I'm flying or waiting in an airport. I'll pull out my knitting and pray for the person I'm making a sweater or a blanket for. It's natural. Being creative is part of worship, I believe. When we are able to use the talents God has given us, that is a worshipful response. Abraham Lincoln said that we may be the only Bible someone reads. Worship is really how we live and carry out our lives.

worship. Not to be legalistic, but to help develop a positive habit. Remember, we're developing those spiritual memory muscles, and the more time we spend in worship with our Father, the more we will enjoy it and desire even more.

Here are a few things that Becky discovered about prayer:

- Prayer fuels faith to dream and hope and risk.
- Prayer "woos" us to the Word by our *need* to hear God's response to our requests.
- Prayer teaches trust in God through

waiting upon *His* timing.

- Prayer reveals God's plan and our purpose in opening up to us detailed directions for both the present and the future.
- Prayer releases God's power to live and walk in the supernatural realm of the Holy Spirit.
- Prayer unleashes love for God — emotional, real and all-consuming.[7]

At the first of the month when I write out my prayers, I have a certain formula I follow. I start with praise and generally take a psalm and rewrite it in my own words, using instances in my life and thanking God for His great goodness to me. Then I follow up with prayers for my husband and children, listing them each by name so that I can usher them before the Lord each morning. This is followed by the three specific people I am praying for each year. Sometimes all I do is list their names. God knows their needs far better than I do. I simply thank Him for bringing these people into my life and ask that they feel a deep spiritual hunger for Him. The list goes on to include my pastor and his family, and our elected officials. The last person I pray for is myself. I ask God to bless my writing. He's the One who gives me my plot ideas. He's the One who lights my path in this world. Then I finish my prayers with praise. Each of us must develop our own pattern for prayer. I share this with you only as a possible outline. Make prayer your own and watch what happens.

In Matthew 6:6, Jesus tells us, "But when you pray, go into your room, close the door and pray to your Father, who is unseen. Then your Father, who sees what is done in secret, will reward you" (NIV).

Hearing God's voice

Worship through prayer is intimate; it's one-on-one with the One who loves us. But talking or writing down our prayers to God is only one part of what our prayer time should be about. We also need to listen to what God wants to say to us.

This can sometimes be confusing. "If I can't hear God's voice, how am I supposed to know what He's telling me?" you may be asking. But God's voice "thunders in marvelous ways," and He does "great things beyond our understanding" (Job 37:5 NIV).

I've never heard God speak in an audible voice, one we can hear like we're talking with a friend or a spouse, although some believe to have heard Him that way. He does speak through His Word; through our thoughts; through our life situations and even through conversations with others. Becky Tirabassi recommends that after writing out our prayers to God, we should ask God to speak to us, and then listen. Write down exactly what you hear in your mind; you will be amazed and blessed at the opportunity of hearing God's voice.

It's natural to doubt that what you've written down, or what you've read in God's Word, is what God is trying to tell you. I recommend that you ask yourself these questions:

- Does what I'm hearing match up with Scripture?
- Does what I'm hearing have the potential of taking me out of my comfort zone? (God has a way of doing that!)
- How am I going to respond to what I believe God is telling me?

When we develop our personal worship and prayer life, when we make an effort to stay involved in corporate worship, we open the opportunity to grow spiritually. That is what God wants from us. He wants our time, He wants our love, and He wants our hearts. He wants our best in everything we do, but, bottom line, He wants our availability.

We were created for purpose. God wants us to learn from Him what our passions are and what our calling is, and He wants us to pursue those things with gusto! As we look toward the future, He also wants us to celebrate the present — He wants us to enjoy this pursuit, this life journey, with enthusiasm and excitement!

We were created for dreams. God longs for us to see our dreams in color, vibrant hues that paint the complete picture of God's plan for us. He wants us to dream big and follow those dreams. He wants us to ignore the lies we and others tell ourselves, and quit putting ourselves in boxes that keep us from achieving our goals. God doesn't put us in a box; let's not put our dreams in a box, either.

We were created for risk. God wants us to take chances and to venture into unknown areas because that is where our faith grows the most. That is where we see God work His miracles, and where we see our obedience rewarded the greatest.

We were created for success. God made us to pursue the purpose and passions He's given us, and we should desire nothing less than achieving those things because when we do, it is God who receives the glory. We need to remember to celebrate the small successes of life as we reach toward accomplishing the bigger things.

We were created for balance. As much as God wants us to succeed, He also wants us to have a balanced spirit. This means putting Him first, putting our family next, our work and our passions after that. It is a more peaceful existence when we have our priorities in the right place.

We were created for relationships. God did not make us to be alone. He wants us to serve together, work together, live together, celebrate one another's joys, and comfort one another in our sorrows.

We were created for the Word. The Bible gives us our hope, for it's through those pages that we can develop our relationship with God. We can learn and grow and improve all the seeds of skills and values He's planted inside us.

We were created for work. God wants us to use the brain and the hands and the feet He's made for us. That means setting goals, looking forward, and listening to God's voice as He guides our way.

We were created for laughter. God desires for us to have joy, to be glad in life's thrills and challenges.

We were created for gratitude. God loves a thankful heart, one that remembers, like the leper, to thank Him for His miracles, to thank Him for His grace that abounds so fully.

We were created for blessing. We were created to be blessed by God and to be a blessing to others.

We were created for worship. We cannot ignore the role of worship when it comes to our relationship with our Creator. He longs for that intimate time with us.

We were created for all these things . . . but most of all, we were created for love. We were created to be loved by God and to love Him back. We were created to love others and to love the life God has given us.

Thank you for sticking with me through *Knit Together*. My prayer is that God has spoken to you personally in these chapters. You are cherished and loved by Him.

Let me close this by restating the Scripture I quoted at the end of the first chapter:

Live creatively, friends. . . . Make a careful exploration of who you are and the work you have been given, and then sink yourself into that. Don't be impressed with yourself. Don't compare yourself with others. Each of you must take responsibility

373

for doing the creative best you can with your own life. (GALATIANS 6:1, 4–5 *THE MESSAGE*)

We each have been knit together by God for a purpose, for a reason. May His handiwork be evident in your life today and throughout the days to come.

NOTES

CHAPTER 1

1. C. S. Lewis, *Surprised by Joy* (Orlando: Harcourt Brace & Company, 1955).
2. Oswald Chambers, *My Utmost for His Highest* (Grand Rapids: Oswald Chambers Publications Association, Ltd., 1992), July 28.

CHAPTER 2

1. Charles Swindoll, *Living Above the Level of Mediocrity* (Nashville: W Publishing Group, 1989), 104.

CHAPTER 3

1. John Ortberg, *If You Want to Walk on Water, You've Got to Get Out of the Boat* (Grand Rapids: Zondervan, 2001), 117–18.
2. Kate White, *Why Good Girls Don't Get Ahead . . . But Gutsy Girls Do* (New York:

Warner Books, 1995), 248.

3. Dr. Norman Vincent Peale, *Power of Positive Thinking* (Upper Saddle River: Prentice-Hall, 1952).

4. Abraham Lincoln, as quoted on www .brainyquote.com (accessed Sept. 25, 2006).

5. John Maxwell, *The Success Journey* (Nashville: Thomas Nelson, 1997), 49.

CHAPTER 4

1. Victor and Mildred Goertzel, *Cradles of Eminence* (New York: Little, Brown & Company, 1962).

2. Brian Tracy, *How to Master Your Time* (Niles: Nightingale-Conart, 1989).

CHAPTER 5

1. Gallup News Service, "Half of Americans Pressed for Time; a Third Are Stressed Out," May 3, 2004.

2. White, *Why Good Girls Don't Get Ahead,* 118.

3. Rick Warren, *The Purpose Driven Life* (Grand Rapids: Zondervan, 2002), 33.

4. Dr. Norman Vincent Peale, *The Power of Positive Thinking* (New York: Random House Publishing Group, 1956), 186–87.

5. Dr. Norman Vincent Peale, as quoted on

www.brainyquote.com (accessed Sept. 25, 2006).

CHAPTER 6

1. Barna Research Group, "Born Again Christians Just As Likely to Divorce As Are Non-Christians," September 8, 2004, http://www.barna.org (accessed 9/22/06).
2. Dr. Emerson Eggerichs, *Love & Respect* (Brentwood: Integrity Publishers, 2004), 29.
3. Taken from a sermon found on Sermon Central.com (accessed Sept. 25, 2006).

CHAPTER 7

1. Robert Frost, as quoted on www.brainy quote.com (accessed Sept. 25, 2006).
2. Voddie Baucham, *The Ever-Loving Truth* (Nashville: B&H Publishing, 2004).
3. George Mueller, *A Narrative of Some of the Lord's Dealings with George Mueller* (Muskegon: Dust and Ashes Publications, 2003).
4. From a sermon illustration found on net .bible.org (accessed Sept. 25, 2006).
5. Charles Swindoll, *Living Insights Study Bible* (Grand Rapids: Zondervan, 1996), 879.

CHAPTER 8

1. Business Owners Toolkit. 1995–2006, CCH Incorporated — a Wolters Kluwer business, http://www.toolkit.cch.com/text/P01_0360.asp (accessed September 29, 2006).
2. Zig Ziglar, *Zig Ziglar's Little Book of Big Quotes.*
3. Ron Blue, *Master Your Money* (Nashville: Thomas Nelson, 1986).
4. Billy Graham, as quoted on SermonCen tral.com (accessed Sept. 25, 2006).

CHAPTER 9

1. Robert R. Provire, "Laughter," *American Scientist* 84.1 (Jan.–Feb., 1996): 38–47. http://cogweb.ucla.edu/Abstracts/Provire_96.html (accessed Sept. 25, 2006).
2. *Today in the Word,* MBI, December 18, 1991.
3. Marshall Brain, "How Laughter Works," HowStuffWorks.com, http://people.how stuffworks.com/laughter7.htm (accessed October 1, 2006).
4. Brett Oppegaard, "Anatomy of a Laugh-Amusing analysis," *Columbian,* Clark County, Washington, September 17, 2006, http://www.columbian.com/lifeHomelife

HomeNews/09172006news59875.cfm (accessed October 1, 2006).

5. PatchAdams.org, "House Calls: Story 10," http://www.patchadams.org/community/house_calls/10.html (accessed October 1, 2006).

6. Judy Siegel-Itzkovich, "Israel sets up course in clowning to help patients recover," *British Medical Journal (BMJ),* October 26, 2002, http://www.pubmed central.nih.gov/articlerender.fcgi?artid= 1169571.

7. Gregg Zoroya, "Pentagon to families: Go ahead, laugh," *USA Today,* January 12, 2006, http://www.usatoday.com/news/washington/2006-01-12-pentagon-laughter_x.htm (accessed October 1, 2006).

8. Charles Swindoll, *Laugh Again* (Nashville: W Publishing, 1992).

9. www.SermonCentral.com.

CHAPTER 10

1. From Jeff Jacoby, "The Power of Giving Thanks," *Boston Globe* staff, 11/23/2000, http://www.homiliesbyemail.com/Special/Thanksgiving/power.txt.

2. Michael E. McCullough and Robert A. Emmons, "How Grateful Are You" Quiz.

(Copyright 2000.) Taken from BeliefNet
.com, http://www.beliefnet.com/section/
quiz/index.asp?sectionID=&surveyID=
105.

3. NIV Study Bible, introduction notes in
the book of Lamentations.

4. Karol Ladd, *The Power of a Positive Mom*
(West Monroe: Howard Publishing,
2001), 131–40.

5. Steve Shepherd in "For Granted or
Gratitude" on www.SermonCentral.com.

6. Bob Russell, "Jesus, Lord of Your Personality," in *Preaching Now Newsletter,* June
25, 2002 (West Monroe: Howard Publishing Co., 2002), 14–16.

CHAPTER 11

1. "The Concept of Grace," taken from
www.SermonCentral.com (accessed October 7, 2006).

2. Philip Yancey, *What's So Amazing About
Grace?* (Grand Rapids, MI: Zondervan,
1997), 70.

3. Allan Luks, "Health Benefits of Kindness-
Abbreviated," *The Healing Power of Doing
Good: The Health and Spiritual Benefits of
Helping Others* (New York: iUniverse.com,
2001), http://www.actsofkindness.org/
inspiration/health/detail.asp?id=2.

4. R. J. Cohn, "Paying it forward comes full circle in Bonner County," Bonner County *Daily Bee,* http://www.bonnercounty dailybee.com/articles/2006/10/07/news/ news03.txt (accessed October 7, 2006).

CHAPTER 12

1. Rev. Dr. Mark D. Roberts in his series *Soul of Worship* at www.markdroberts .com. "Tethered Creativity: Worship and the Word of God," copyright 2004, http://www.markdroberts.com/htmfiles/ resources/soulworship.htm.
2. James Pittman, *What Is Worship?,* managing editor, David Sper (Grand Rapids, MI: RBC Ministries, 1987, 2001).
3. Charles Colson, *How Now Shall We Live?* (Wheaton: Tyndale, 1999), 14–15.
4. Pittman, *What Is Worship?,* 18.
5. Albert L. Winseman, "Friendship Feeds the Flock," Gallup poll, April 26, 2005, www.galluppoll.com.
6. Jill Briscoe, "Heart to Heart," *Today's Christian Woman.*
7. Becky Tirabassi, *Let Prayer Change Your Life* (Nashville: Thomas Nelson, 1990, 1992, 2000), 134–35.

ACKNOWLEDGMENTS

Scripture quotations noted NIV are from the HOLY BIBLE, NEW INTERNA-TIONAL VERSION®. Copyright © 1973, 1978, 1984 by International Bible Society. Used by permission of Zondervan Publishing House. All rights reserved.

The "NIV" and "New International Version" trademarks are registered in the United States Patent and Trademark Office by International Bible Society. Use of either trademark requires the permission of International Bible Society.

Scripture quotations noted *The Message* are from *THE MESSAGE.* Copyright © 1993, 1994, 1995, 1996, 2000, 2001, 2002. Used by permission of NavPress Publishing Group.

Scripture quotations noted NKJV are from THE NEW KING JAMES VERSION OF THE BIBLE. Copyright © 1979, 1980, 1982, Thomas Nelson, Inc., Publishers.

ABOUT THE AUTHOR

With more than 60 million copies of her books in print, *New York Times* bestselling author **Debbie Macomber** is a leading voice in women's fiction worldwide. Writing stories about towns people love and characters they long remember, Debbie offices in a Victorian-style building that also houses an ice cream parlor and a bookstore. The Washington native and mother of four grown children is known for her heartwarming stories about small-town life, home and family values, women who knit, enduring friendships, and humorous angels named Shirley, Goodness, and Mercy, three prayer ambassadors who tackle their earthly missions with zeal. She demonstrates an almost uncanny ability to see into the hearts of women and to express their emotions, values, and concerns.

Many of Debbie's novels are set in small towns based on her own Port Orchard, WA.

One of those novels, *44 Cranberry Point,* was voted the national "readers' choice" Quill Award in 2006. Her most recent *New York Times* bestselling novels are *Susannah's Garden* and *A Good Yarn.*

Debbie serves on the national advisory board for *Guideposts* magazine, for which she also writes devotionals. She begins each day at 4 a.m., when she reads her Bible, studies her craft, writes in her gratitude journal — and then swims a half-mile before reporting to her office to write the books of her heart.

The employees of Thorndike Press hope you have enjoyed this Large Print book. All our Thorndike and Wheeler Large Print titles are designed for easy reading, and all our books are made to last. Other Thorndike Press Large Print books are available at your library, through selected bookstores, or directly from us.

For information about titles, please call:
(800) 223-1244

or visit our Web site at:
http://gale.cengage.com/thorndike

To share your comments, please write:
Publisher
Thorndike Press
295 Kennedy Memorial Drive
Waterville, ME 04901